Our India

Population (2011)	: 1,21,08,54,977
Capital	: New Delhi
Area	: 32,87,263 sq km
Geographic Location	: Between 8°4' and 37°6' north latitudes; Between 68°7' and 97°25' east longitudes
Coastline Length	: 7,516.6 km including the coastline of Lakshadweep, Andaman & Nicobar Islands.
Number of States	: 28*
Number of Union Territories	: 9
Major Languages	: 22
National Anthem	: Jana Gana Mana
National Currency	: Rupee (₹)
National Animal	: Tiger
National Aquatic Animal	: Dolphin
National Bird	: Peacock
National River	: Ganga
Characteristics of Indian Legislature	: Socialist, Secular, Democratic, Republic; Bicameral Legislature at the Centre; Uni/Bicameral Legislatures in States
Executive	: President, Vice-President and Council of Ministers at the Centre; Governor and Council of Ministers in States
Judiciary	: Independent from Executive with Supreme Court at the apex of the hierarchy
Total Road Length	: 56.17 lakh kilometres at Present

* After bifurcation of Jammu & Kashmir into two Union Territories J&K and Ladakh in August 2019.

(R-1641) GK–1

India: States & Union Territories

States/Union Territories	Capital	Area in (Sq. Km.)	Language
Andhra Pradesh	Hyderabad	160,229	Telugu
Arunachal Pradesh	Itanagar	83,743	Nyishi, Miji, Wancho etc.
Assam	Dispur	78,438	Assamese
Bihar	Patna	94,163	Hindi, Maithili
Chhattisgarh	Raipur	137,898	Hindi
Goa	Panji	3,702	Marathi and Konkani
Gujarat	Gandhinagar	1,96,024	Gujarati
Haryana	Chandigarh	44,212	Hindi
Himachal Pradesh	Shimla	55,673	Hindi and Pahari
Jharkhand	Ranchi	79,714	Hindi, Santhali
Karnataka	Bengaluru	1,91,791	Kannada
Kerala	Thiruvananthapuram	38,863	Malayalam
Madhya Pradesh	Bhopal	308,000	Hindi
Maharashtra	Mumbai	307,713	Marathi
Manipur	Imphal	22,327	Manipuri
Meghalaya	Shillong	22,429	Khasi, Garo and English
Mizoram	Aizawl	21,081	Mizo and English
Nagaland	Kohima	16,579	Sema, English
Odisha	Bhubaneswar	155,707	Odiya
Punjab	Chandigarh	50,362	Punjabi
Rajasthan	Jaipur	3,42,239	Hindi and Rajasthani
Sikkim	Gangtok	7,096	Bhutia, Nepali, Lepcha and Limbu
Tamil Nadu	Chennai	1,30,058	Tamil
Telangana	Hyderabad	1,14,840	Telugu
Tripura	Agartala	10,491	Bengali, Kakborak, Manipuri
Uttar Pradesh	Lucknow	2,40,928	Hindi and Urdu
Uttarakhand	Dehradun	53,483	Hindi
West Bengal	Kolkata	88,752	Bengali
Andaman & Nicobar Island	Port Blair	8,249	Bengali, Hindi, Nicobarese, Tamil, Telugu, and Malayalam
Chandigarh	Chandigarh	114	Hindi, Punjabi
Dadara and Nagar Haveli	Silvassa	491	Gujarati and Hindi
Daman and Diu	Daman	112	Gujarati
Delhi	Delhi	1483	Hindi, Punjabi and Urdu
Lakshadweep	Kavaratti	32	Malayalam
Puducherry	Puducherry	479	Tamil, Telugu, Malayalam, English and French
Jammu & Kashmir*	Srinagar (Summer) Jammu (Winter)	2,22,236	Kashmiri, Urdu, Dogri
Ladakh	—	—	—

* Data of Ladakh is included in it.

Population

Second Largest Nation : In terms of the size of population, India is the second largest country in the world, next only to China. China tops the list with 1380.0 million people. India's population constitutes nearly 17.5 per cent of the total world population while her geographical area is only 2.42 per cent of the world area. With such a huge population to support on so small an area, the country finds herself in great difficulty in making any significant dent on its poverty and economic backwardness. India's national income, which is barely 2 per cent of the total global income, clearly shows the tremendous strain of population on her economy.

2011 CENSUS HIGHLIGHTS

Population of India—Total Indian population is 17.7% of total world population	:	1,21,08,54,977 (Male: 62,32,70,258; Female: 58,75,84,719)
Decadal Growth (2001-2011)	:	17.7 per cent (Males: 17.1 per cent; Females: 18.3 per cent)
Highest Decadal Growth (State-wise)	:	Meghalaya (27.9 per cent)
Lowest Decadal Growth (State-wise)	:	Nagaland (–0.6 per cent)
Most populous State	:	Uttar Pradesh (16.17 per cent of National Population)
Density of population	:	382 persons per sq. km.
Most densly populated State	:	Bihar : 1106 per sq. km
Sex Ratio	:	943 females per 1000 males
Total Literacy Rate	:	73% (Males – 80.9%) (Females – 64.06%)
Highest Literacy (State-wise)	:	Kerala (94%)
Lowest Literacy (State-wise)	:	Bihar (61.8)

Other Details

(a) Population of India

1951	36,10,88,090	1961	43,92,34,771
1971	54,81,59,652	1981	68,33,29,097
1991	84,64,21,039	2001	102,87,37,436
2011	1,21,08,54,977		

(b) Density of Population (Persons per square kilometre)

1951	113	1961	138
1971	177	1981	216
1991	267	2001	324
2011	382		

(c) Annual Compound Rate of Growth

1941-1951	1.25 per cent	1951-1961	1.96 per cent
1961-1971	2.22 per cent	1971-1981	2.20 per cent
1981-1991	2.14 per cent	1991-2001	1.95 per cent
2001-2011	1.64 per cent		

2011 CENSUS OF INDIA : POPULATION DISTRIBUTION, POPULATION DENSITY AND LITERACY RATE

S. No.	State/ Union Territories*	Population 2011			Population Density (per sq. km.)	Literacy Rate 2011		
		Persons	Males	Females	2011	Persons	Males	Females
	INDIA	1,21,08,54,977	62,32,70,258	58,75,84,719	382	73.0	80.9	64.6
1.	Jammu and Kashmir	1,25,41,302	66,40,662	59,00,640	124	67.2	76.8	56.4
2.	Himachal Pradesh	68,64,602	34,81,873	33,82,729	123	82.8	89.5	75.9
3.	Punjab	2,77,43,338	1,46,39,465	1,31,03,873	551	75.8	80.4	70.7
4.	Chandigarh*	10,55,450	5,80,663	4,74,787	9,258	86.0	90.0	81.2
5.	Uttarakhand	1,00,86,292	51,37,773	49,48,519	189	78.8	87.4	70.0
6.	Haryana	2,53,51,462	1,34,94,734	1,18,56,728	573	75.6	84.1	65.9
7.	Delhi*	1,67,87,941	89,87,326	78,00,615	11,320	86.2	90.9	80.8
8.	Rajasthan	6,85,48,437	3,55,50,997	3,29,97,440	200	66.1	79.2	52.1
9.	Uttar Pradesh	19,98,12,341	10,44,80,510	9,53,31,831	829	67.7	77.3	57.2
10.	Bihar	10,40,99,452	5,42,78,157	4,98,21,295	1,106	61.8	71.2	51.5
11.	Sikkim	6,10,577	3,23,070	2,87,507	86	81.4	86.6	75.6
12.	Arunachal Pradesh	13,83,727	7,13,912	6,69,815	17	65.4	72.6	57.7
13.	Nagaland	19,78,502	10,24,649	9,53,853	119	79.6	82.8	76.1
14.	Manipur	28,55,794	14,38,586	14,17,208	128	76.94	83.58	70.26
15.	Mizoram	10,97,206	5,55,339	5,41,867	52	91.3	93.3	89.3
16.	Tripura	36,73,917	18,74,376	17,99,541	350	87.2	91.5	82.7
17.	Meghalya	29,66,889	14,91,832	14,75,057	132	74.4	76.0	72.9
18.	Assam	3,12,05,576	1,59,39,443	1,52,66,133	398	72.2	77.8	66.3
19.	West Bengal	9,12,76,115	4,68,09,027	4,44,67,088	1,028	76.3	81.7	70.5
20.	Jharkhand	3,29,88,134	1,69,30,315	1,60,57,819	414	66.4	76.8	55.4
21.	Odisha	4,19,74,218	2,12,12,136	2,07,62,082	270	72.9	81.6	64.0
22.	Chhattisgarh	2,55,45,198	1,28,32,895	1,27,12,303	189	70.3	80.3	60.2
23.	Madhya Pradesh	7,26,26,809	3,76,12,306	3,50,14,503	236	69.3	78.7	59.2
24.	Gujarat	6,04,39,692	3,14,91,260	2,89,48,432	308	78.0	85.8	69.7
25.	Daman and Diu*	2,43,247	1,50,301	92,946	2,191	87.1	91.5	79.5
26.	Dadra & Nagar Haweli*	3,43,709	1,93,760	1,49,949	700	76.2	85.2	64.3
27.	Maharashtra	11,23,74,333	5,82,43,056	5,41,31,277	365	82.3	88.4	75.9
28.	Andhra Pradesh	4,93,86,799	2,47,38,068	2,46,48,731	308	67.4	74.8	60.0
29.	Karnataka	6,10,95,297	3,09,66,657	3,01,28,640	319	75.4	82.5	68.1
30.	Goa	14,58,545	7,39,140	7,19,405	394	88.7	92.6	84.7
31.	Lakshadweep*	64,473	33,123	31,350	2,149	91.8	95.6	87.9
32.	Kerala	3,34,06,061	1,60,27,412	1,73,78,649	860	94.0	96.1	92.1
33.	Tamil Nadu	7,21,47,030	3,61,37,975	3,60,09,055	555	80.1	86.8	73.4
34.	Puducherry*	12,47,953	6,12,511	6,35,442	2,547	85.8	91.3	80.7
35.	Andaman & Nicobar Island*	3,80,581	2,02,871	1,77,710	46	86.6	90.3	82.4
36.	Telangana	3,51,93,978	17,704,078	17,489,900	308	66.5	75.0	57.9

National Symbols

National Emblem: State emblem of India is an adaptation from the Sarnath Lion Capital of Ashoka. It was adopted by the Government of India on January 26, 1950. In the adapted form, only three lions are visible, the fourth being hidden from the view. The wheel (Dharma Chakra) appears in relief in the centre of the abacus with a bull on the right and a horse on the left. The bell-shaped lotus has been omitted. The words "Satyameva Jayate" meaning "Truth alone triumphs" are inscribed below the Emblem in Devanagari script. 

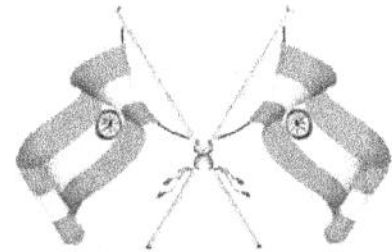

National Flag: The National Flag of India is a horizontal tricolour of deep saffron (Kesari), white and dark green in equal proportion. In the centre of the white band there is a wheel in navy blue colour. It has 24 spokes. The ratio of the length and the breadth of the flag is 3 : 2. Its design was adopted by the Constituent Assembly of India on July 22, 1947.

National Anthem: Rabindranath Tagore's song 'Jana-gana-mana' was adopted by the Constituent Assembly as the National Anthem of India on January 24, 1950.

Jana-gan-mana-adhinayaka jaya he, Bharata-bhagya-vidhata
Punjab-Sindh-Gujarat-Maratha-Dravida-Utkala-Banga
Vindhya-Himachala-Yamuna-Ganga Uchhala-jaladhi-taranga.
Tava subha name jage, Tava subha asisa mange, Gahe tava jaya gatha,
Jana-gana-mangala-dayak, jaya he Bharata bhagya vidhata,
Jaya he, jaya he, jaya he, Jaya jaya jaya, jaya he.

National Song: Bankim Chandra Chatterji's 'Vande Mataram' which was a source of inspiration to the people in their struggle for freedom, has been adopted as National Song. It has an equal status with the National Anthem.

Vande Mataram
Sujalam, suphalam, malayaja-shitalam,
Shasya shyamalam, Mataram
Shubhrajyotsna,pulkita yaminim,
Phulla kusumita drumadalashobhinim,
Subhasinim sumadhura—bhashinim,
Sukhadam, Varadam, Mataram.

National Bird and Animal of India: Peacock and Tiger; **National Aquatic Animal:** Dolphin; **National Flower:** Lotus; **National Game:** Hockey; **National Calendar:** It was adopted on March 22, 1957. It has 365 days in the year and the first month of the year is Chaitra.

Months of the National Calendar: (1) Chaitra, (2) Vaishakha, (3) Jaishtha, (4) Ashadha, (5) Shravan, (6) Bhadra, (7) Ashvina, (8) Kartika, (9) Marga-Shirsha, (10) Pausha, (11) Magha, (12) Phalguna. ❏❏

The Universe

The Solar System: Some Facts

Number of Planets: 8—Mercury, Venus, Earth, Mars, Jupiter, Saturn, Uranus and Neptune.

Largest most

Massive planet	Jupiter	Most circular orbit	Venus
Brightest planet	Venus	Shortest (synodic) day	Jupiter
Brightest star	Sirius	Hottest planet	Venus
Fastest orbiting planet	Mercury	No moons	Mercury, Venus
Longest (Synodic) day	Mercury	Planet with moon with most eccentric orbit	Neptune
Most moons	Jupiter-67		
Planet with largest moon	Jupiter		
Greatest average density	Jupiter	Lowest average density	Saturn
Tallest mountain	Earth	Greatest amount of liquid on the surface	Earth
Strongest magnetic fields	Jupiter		

The Earth: Facts and Data

Composition of the Earth: Aluminium (0.4%), Sulphur (2.7%), Silicon (13%), Oxygen (28%), Calcium (1.2%), Nickel (2.7%), Magnesium (17%), Iron (35%)

Surface area	: 510100500 sq km	Polar radius	: 6335 km
Land Surface (29.1%)	: 148950800 sq km	Mass (estimated weight)	: 594×10^{19} metric tons
Ocean Surface (70.9%)	: 361149700 sq km	Mean distance from the Sun	: 149407000 km
Type of water	: 97% salt, 3% fresh	Earth's orbit speed (around sun)	: 107320 kmph
Total area of water	: 382672000 sq km	Period of Revolution (round the sun)	: 365 days 5 hrs 48 min. 45.51 seconds
Equatorial diameter	: 12753 km	Time of Rotation (on its axis)	: 23 hrs 56 min. 4.09 seconds
Equatorial Circumference	: 40066 km		
Polar Circumference	: 39992 km	Inclination of the axis (to the plane of the eclipitc)	: 23º27'
Polar diameter	: 12710 km		
Equatorial radius	: 6376 km		

Solar Statistics

Distance from the Earth	: 149.8 million km	from the Earth (near the poles)	: 33 days
Absolute Visual Magnitude	: 4.75	Chemical Composition	: Hydrogen 71% Helium 26.5% Other elements 2.5%
Diameter Core Temperature	: 1,384,000 km : 15000000 K		
Photosphere Temperature	: 5770 K		
Rotation as seen from the Earth (at the equator)	: 25.38 days	Age	: About 4.5 billion years
Rotation as seen		Expected lifetime of a normal star	: About 10 billion years

Oceans of the World

Pacific	166,241,000 sq km	Indian	73,427,000 sq km
Atlantic	86,557,000 sq km	Arctic	9,485,000 sq km

Longest Rivers

Name	Country/ Continent	Length in Kilometres	Name	Country/ Continent	Length in Kilometres
Nile	Africa	6650	Niger	Africa	4180
Amazon	S. America	6437	St. Lawrence	Canada (USA)	4023
Mississippi-Missouri	USA	6020	Murray-Darling	Australia	3780
Yangtze-Kiang	China	5494	Volga	Russia	3690
Ob-Irtysh	Russia	5410	Indus	Asia	2900
Lena	Russia	4400	Danube	Europe	2850
Hwang Ho	China	4344	Orinoco	S. America	2575

Major Riverside Cities

City	River	Country	City	River	Country
Alexandria	Nile	Egypt	Lahore	Ravi	Pakistan
Amsterdam	Amsel	Netherland	Lisbon	Tagus	Portugal
Ankara	Kizil	Turkey	Liverpool	Mersey	England
Baghdad	Tigris	Iraq	London	Thames	England
Bangkok	Menam	Thailand	Moscow New	Moskva	Russia
Belgrade	Danube	Yugoslavia	Orleans	Mississipi	USA
Berlin	Spree	Germany	New York	Hudson	USA
Budapest	Danube	Hungary	Paris	Seine	France
Cairo	Nile	Egypt	Rangoon (Yangon)	Irawadi	Myanmar
Chittagong	Karnaphuli	Bangladesh			
Karachi	Indus	Pakistan			
Khartoum	Blue & White Nile	Sudan	Rome	Tiber	Italy

Major Gulfs of the World

Names	Areas (Sq. Km.)	Names	Areas (Sq. Km.)
Gulf of Mexico	15,44,000	Gulf of St. Lawrence	2,37,000
Gulf of Hudson	12,33,000	Gulf of California	1,62,000
Arabian Gulf	2,38,000	English Channel	89,900

Major Mountain Ranges of the World

Range	Location	Length (km)
Andes	South America	7,200
Himalayas-Karakoram-Hindukush	South Central Asia	5,000
Rockies	North America	4,800
Great Dividing Range	East Australia	3,600
Atlas	North West Africa	1,930
Western Ghats	Western India	1,610
Caucasus	Europe	1,200
Alaska	USA	1,130
Alps	Europe	1,050

Largest Deserts of the World

Subtropical

Sahara, North Africa	94,00,000 sq. km.
Kalahari, Southern Africa	582,727 sq. km.
Thar, India/Pakistan	2,00,000 sq. km.
Great Sandy, Australia	4,00,000 sq. km.

Cool Coastal

Atacama, Chile S.A.	1,40,000 sq. km

Cool Winter

Gobi, China	13,00,000 sq. km.
Colorado, Western USA	3,37,000 sq. km.

(also called the painted desert)

Atmosphere

Composition of Gases in Atmosphere

Nitrogen	78.03%	Neon	0.0018%
Oxygen	20.99%	Helium	0.0005%
Argon	0.93%	Crypton	0.0001%
Carbon dioxide	0.03%	Xenon	0.000,005%
Hydrogen	0.01%	Ozone	0.000,0001%

World Important Local Winds

Chinoon: A warm day wind frequently experienced on the eastern side of the Rocky Mountains.

Fohn: A warm dry wind descending a mountain, as on the north side of the Alps.

Haboob: A sand storm or a dust storm in north and north-east Sudan near Khartoum.

Bagrrio: It is the tropical cyclone of the Philippine Island.

Loo: A hot wind which blows in summer season in Indian sub-continent.

Papasago: A cold northerly wind sometimes felt on the Mexico plateau.

Bora: It is the name given to the cold dry wind experienced particularly in winter along the eastern coast of the Atlantic Ocean and in northern Italy.

Black Toller: A hot dust wind which blows in the vast plain of North America.

Principal Mountain Peaks of the World

Mountains	Height in Metres	Range	Date of First Ascent
1. Mount Everest	8,848	Himalayas	May 29, 1953
2. K-2 (Godwin Austen)	8,611	Karakoram	July 31, 1954
3. Kanchenjunga	8,597	Himalayas	May 25, 1955
4. Lhotse	8,511	Himalayas	May 18, 1956
5. Makalu I	8,481	Himalayas	May 15, 1955
6. Dhaulagiri I	8,167	Himalayas	May 13, 1960
7. Mansalu I	8,156	Himalayas	May 9, 1956
8. Chollyo	8,153	Himalayas	Oct. 19, 1954
9. Nanga Parbat	8,124	Himalayas	July 3, 1953
10. Annapurna I	8,091	Himalayas	June 3, 1950
11. Gasherbrum I	8,068	Karakoram	July 5, 1958
12. Broad Peak I	8,047	Karakoram	June 9, 1957
13. Gasherbrum II	8,034	Karakoram	July 7, 1956
14. Shisha Pangma (Gosainthan)	8,014	Himalayas	May 2, 1964
15. Gasherbrum III	7,952	Karakoram	Aug. 11, 1975

Types of World Agriculture

Viticulture: The cultivation of the vine for production of grapes and wine.

Pisciculture: The breeding, rearing and transplantation of fish by artificial means.

Sericulture: The raising of silk worms for the production of raw silk.

Horticulture: To grow flower front, vegetables on small plots.

Apiculture: Bee keeping on a commercial scale for the sale of honey.

Floriculture: The cultivation of flowers or flowering plants.

Mariculture: Sea farming, or the cultivation of marine plants and animals for commercial purposes.

Olericulture: The cultivation of vegetables and kitchen herbs.

Famous Straits of the World

Strait	Between	Country
Malacca Strait	Andaman Sea and South China Sea	Indonesia
Palk Strait	Mannar and Bay of Bengal	India-Sri Lanka
Magellan Strait	Pacific and South Atlantic Ocean	Chile
Dover Strait	English Channel and North Sea	England-France
Berring Strait	Berring Sea and Chukasi Sea	Alaska-Russia
Sugaroo Strait	Japan Sea and Pacific Ocean	Japan
Sunda Strait	Java and Indian Ocean	Indonesia
Gibralter Strait	Mediterranean Sea and Atlantic Ocean	Spain
Harmuj Strait	Persia and Bay of Oman	Oman-Iran
Hudson Strait	Bay of Hudson and Atlantic Ocean	Canada

World's Famous Official Documents

White Paper: India; **Orange Book:** Netherlands; **Yellow Book:** France; **Green Book:** Italy and Iran; **White Book:** Portugal, China and Germany; **Grey Book:** Japan and Belgium.

Famous Newspapers of the World

News-paper	Place of Publishing	Language	News-paper	Place of Publishing	Language
Daily News	New York (America)	English	Daily Mirror	Britain	English
Guardian	London (Britain)	English	Hindu, Hindustan Times, Times of India, Tribune, Statesman, Indian Express, Economic Times	India	English
Pravada	Moscow (Russia)	Russian			
Al-Ahram	Cairo (Egypt)	Arabic			
Merdeca	Jakarta (Indonesia)	Indonesian			
Times	London (Britain)	English	Hindustan, Nav Bharat Times, Rashtriya Sahara, Dainik Jagaran, Punjab Kesari	India	Hindi
People's Daily	Beijing (China)	Chinese			
New Statesman	Britain	English			

Important Boundary Lines

Boundary Line	Countries	Boundary Line	Countries
Hindenberg Line	Germany-Poland	Durand Line	Pakistan and Afghanistan
Maginot Line	France and Germany	17th Parallel	The line which defined the boundary between North Vietnam and South Vietnam before the two were united.
Mannerhein Line	Russia-Finland		
Mc Mahon Line	India and China		
Order Niesse Line	Germany-Poland	38th Parallel	North Korea and South Korea
Radcliff Line	India-Pakistan		
Seigfrid Line	Germany-France	49th Parallel	U.S.A. and Canada

Areawise 10 Big and Small Countries

10 Big Countries

S. No.	Country	Sq. km (Area)	S. No.	Country	Sq. km (Area)
1.	Russia (Europe-Asia)	17,098,242	6.	Australia (S. Pacific)	77,41,220
2.	Canada (N. America)	99,84,670	7.	India (Asia)	32,87,263
3.	China (Asia)	95,96,961	8.	Argentina (S. America)	27,80,400
4.	U.S.A. (N. America)	93,72,614	9.	Kazakhstan (Europe-Asia)	27,24,900
5.	Brazil (S. America)	85,14,877	10.	Algeria (Africa)	23,81,741

10 Small Countries

S.N.	Country	Area (Sq. km)	S.N.	Country	Area (Sq. km)
1.	Vatican City (Europe)	0.44	7.	Marshall Island (Central Pacific)	181.00
2.	Monaco (Europe)	1.95			
3.	Nauru (Southern Pacific)	21.10	8.	St. Kitts and Nevis (Eastern Caribbean)	261.00
4.	Tuvalu	26.00			
5.	San Marino (Europe)	61.00	9.	Grenada (Eastern Caribbean Sea)	344.00
6.	Liechtenstein (Europe)	160.00	10.	Seychelles (Indian Ocean)	455.00

Populationwise 10 Big and Small Countries

10 Big Countries

S. No.	Country	Population (2017) (In crore)	S. No.	Country	Population (2017) (In crore)
1.	China (Asia)	138.0	6.	Pakistan (Asia)	20.49
2.	India (Asia)	128.1	7.	Nigeria (Africa)	19.06
3.	U.S.A. (North America)	32.66	8.	Bangladesh (Asia)	15.78
4.	Indonesia (Asia)	26.58	9.	Russia (Europe-Asia)	14.25
5.	Brazil (South America)	20.73	10.	Japan (Asia)	12.64

10 Small Countries

S. No.	Country	Population (2017)	S. No.	Country	Population (2017)
1.	Vatican City (Europe)	1000	7.	Liechstein (Europe)	38,244
2.	Nauru (Southern Pacific)	9,642	8.	St. Kitts and Nevis (Eastern Caribbean)	52,715
3.	Tuvalu (Southern Pacific)	11,052			
4.	Palau (Western Pacific)	21,431	9.	Marshall Island (Central Pacific)	74,539
5.	Monaco (Europe)	30,645			
6.	San Marino (Europe)	33,537	10.	Andora (Europe)	85,702

Signals/Signs and Meaning

Signal/Sign	Meaning	Signal/Sign	Meaning
Red Triangle	Family Planning	White Flag	Treaty or Surrender
Red Cross	Medical Help	Yellow Flag	Vehicles with patients of contagious diseases
Red Light	Danger, 'Stop' for the movement of vehicles		
Green Light	Go	Two Bones across with a Skull	Danger of electricity
Olive Branch	Peace	Half mast flown Flag	National mourning
White Pigeon or Dove	Peace	Lotus	Sign of civilization and culture
Black Strip on Arm	(i) Opposition (ii) Sorrow	Wheel (Chakra)	Sign of Progress
Black Flag	Opposition	A blind folded woman with scale in hand	Sign of Justice
Red Flag	(i) Danger (ii) Revolution	Reversed flown	National calamity flag

National Emblems of Important Countries

Country	National Emblem	Country	National Emblem
America	Golden Rod	New Zealand	Kiwi, Fern
Australia	Kangaroo		Southern Cross
Ireland	Shamrock	Norway	Lion
Italy	White Lily	Nepal	Kukri
Israel	Candelabrum	Pakistan	Crescent
Iran	Rose	Poland	Eagle
Canada	White Lily	France	Lily
Great Britain	Rose	Belgium	Lion
Chile	Candor and Huemul	Bangladesh	Water Lily
Germany	Corn Flower	Mongolia	The Soyombo
Japan	Chrysanthemum	Russia	Double headed eagle
Zimbabwe	Zimbabwe Bird	Lebanon	Cedar Tree
Denmark	Beach	Sudan	Secretary Bird
Turkey	Crescent and Star	Syria	Eagle
The Netherlands	Lion	India	Lioned Capital

The Continents of the World

Name	Area (In sq. km.)	Population (2017) (In million)	Per cent of the World's Population
Asia	31,845,872	4,404	59.5
Africa	30,195,394	1,222	16.5
Europe	23,064,084	747	10.1
North America	24,398,475	362	4.9
South America	17,808,695	630	8.5
Australia	8,525,391	38.002	0.5
Antarctica	14,200,000	—	—

International Date Line

It roughly corresponds to 180°E or W meridian of longitude which falls on the opposite side of the Greenwich meridian and the date changes by one day (i.e. 24 hours), as this line is crossed. On crossing this line from east to west a day is added, and a day is subtracted on crossing it from west to east.

General Knowledge

United Nations Organisation

- **Origin:** UN Charter was signed by 50 members on June 26, 1945. It officially came into existence on October 24, 1945.
- **UN Charter:** The Charter is the Constitution of the UNO and contains its aims and objectives and rules and regulations for its functioning.
- **Aims and Objectives:** They are security, welfare and human rights.
- **Headquarters:** New York.
- **Flag:** The flag is light blue in colour, and emblazoned in white, in its centre is the UN symbol—a polar map of world embraced by twin olive branches open at the top.
- **Official Languages:** The official languages of the UN are: English, French, Chinese, Russian, Arabic and Spanish. However, working languages are English & French only.

Secretary General of the U.N.O.

Name	Country	Tenure
Trygve Lie	Norway	(1946-53)
Dog Hammarsk-joeld	Sweden	(1953-61)
U. Thant	Myanmar	(1961-71)
Kurt Waldheim	Austria	(1972-81)
Javier Perez de Cuellar	Peru	(1982-91)
Dr. Boutros Ghali	Egypt	(1992-96)
Kofi Annan	Ghana	(1997-2006)
Ban Ki-moon	South Korea	(2007-2016)
Anonio Guterres	Portugal	(2017- ------)

- **Main Organs of the UNO:** There are six main organs:
  1. General Assembly
  2. Security Council
  3. Economic and Social Council
  4. Trusteeship Council
  5. International Court of Justice, and (6) Secretariat.
  1. **General Assembly:** It consists of representative of all members of the UN. Each member country has only one vote. It meets once a year and passes UN Budget.
  2. **Security Council:** It is the Executive body of the UN and is mainly responsible for maintaining international peace and security. It has 15 members, 5 of which (USA, UK, France, Russia and China) are permanent members. The 10 non-permanent members are elected by General Assembly for two-year term and are not eligible for immediate re-election.
  3. **Economic and Social Council:** It has 54 members elected by General Assembly.
  4. **Trusteeship Council:** It looks after interest of the people in areas not yet independent and leads them towards self-government.

5. **International Court of Justice:** It has 15 judges, no two of whom may be nationals of the same state. They are elected by General Assembly and Security Council for a term of 9 years. The Court elects its President and Vice-President for a 3-year term.
6. **Secretariat:** It is the Secretariat of the UN and is headed by the Secretary General.

Years Observed by United Nations Organisation

1967 : International Tourism Year	2000 : Year of the Culture of Peace
1968 : Human Rights Year	2001 : International Year of Volunteer
1970 : International Education Year	2002 : International Year of Eco-tourism
1972 : International Book Year	2003 : International Year of Fresh Water
1973 : Copernicus Year	2004 : International Rice Year
1974 : World Population Year	2005 : International Year of Sports and Physical Education
1975 : International Women's Year	
1979 : International Year of the Child	2006 : International Year of Deserts and Desertification
1981 : International Year of Disabled	
1983 : World Communication Year	2008 : International Year of Potato
1985 : International Youth Year	2009 : International Year of Astronomy
1986 : International Year of Peace	2010 : International Year of Bio-diversity
1987 : International Year of Shelter for the Homeless	2011 : International Year of Forest
	2012 : International Year of Cooperatives
1990 : International Literacy Year	2013 : International Year of Water Cooperation
1992 : International Space Year	
1993 : International Year for World's Indigenous People	2014 : International Year of Family Farming
	2015 : International Year of Soils
1994 : International Year of Family	2016 : International Year of Pulses
1995 : International Year of Tolerance	2017 : International Year of Sustainable Tourism for Development
1996 : International Year for Eradication of Poverty	
1998 : Human Rights Year	2019 : International year of Indigenous Languages.
1999 : Year of Older Persons	

- **Present Membership:** At present 193 countries are members of the UNO. South Sudan is the latest entrant to this world organisation.

Famous International Organisations, Headquarters and Year of Establishment

International Organisations	Headquarters	Year of Establishment
United Nations Organisations (U.N.O.)	New York	1945
International Monetary Fund (I.M.F.)	Washington	1945
World Health Organisation (W.H.O.)	Geneva	1948
Food & Agricultural Organisation (FAO)	Rome	1943
International Labour Organisation (ILO)	Geneva	1919
UNESCO	Paris	1946
International Court of Justice	The Hague	—
Universal Postal Union (UPU)	Berne	1874
International Civil Aviation Organisation (ICAO)	Montreal	1947
UNIDO	Vienna	1967
International Atomic Energy Agency (IAEA)	Vienna	1957
International Finance Corporation (IFC)	Washington	1956
United Nations Development Programme (UNDP)	New York	—
UNICEF	New York	1946

International Organisations	Headquarters	Year of Establishment
International Maritime Organisation (IMO)	London	1948
World Meteorological Organisation (WMO)	Geneva	1951
International Telecommunication Union (ITU)	Geneva	1947
Arab League	Cairo	1945
Commonwealth of Nations	London	1931
World Trade Organisation (WTO)	Geneva	1995
International Development Association (IDA)	Washington D.C.	1960
International Bank for Reconstruction and Development (IBRD)	Washington D.C.	1946
World Intellectual Property Organisation (WIPO)	Geneva	1967
Organisation of Islamic Cooperation (OIC)	Jeddah (Saudi Arabia)	1971
European Economic Community (EEC)	Geneva	1957
Red Cross	Geneva	1863
Interpol	Lyons	1923
Asian Development Bank (ADB)	Manila	1966
North Atlantic Treaty Organisation (NATO)	Brussels	1949
Association of South East Asian Nations (ASEAN)	Jakarta	1967
South Asian Association for Regional Cooperation (SAARC)	Kathmandu	1985
Asia-Pacific Economic Cooperation (APEC)	–	1989
Organisation for Economic Cooperation and Development (OECD)	Paris	1961
Organisation of Petroleum Exporting Countries (OPEC)	Vienna	1960
Common Wealth of Independent States (CIS)	Minsk	1991
International Olympic Committee (IOC)	Switzerland	1894
European Union (EU)	Brussels	1965
Amnesty International (AI)	London	1961
Shanghai Cooperation Organisation (SCO)	–	2002

Defence

The Supreme Command of the Armed Forces is vested in the hands of the President of the Country. The responsibility for national defence, however, rests with the Cabinet. All important questions having a bearing on defence are decided by the Cabinet Committee on Political Affairs, which is presided over by the Prime Minister. The Defence Minister is responsible to Parliament for all matters concerning the Defence Services. All the administrative and operational control of Armed Forces are exercised by the Ministry of Defence. The three services – Army, Navy and Air Force function through their respective service headquarters headed by the chief of Staff.

Commissioned Ranks in Defence Services

Army	Navy	Air Force
General	Admiral	Air Chief Marshal
Lieutenant-General	Vice-Admiral	Air Marshal
Major-General	Rear-Admiral	Air Vice-Marshal
Brigadier	Commodor	Air Commodor
Colonel	Captain	Group Captain
Lieutenant-Colonel	Commander	Wing Commander
Major	Lt.Commander	Squadron Leader
Captain	Lieutenant	Flight Lieutenant
Lieutenant	Sub-Lieutenant	Flying Officer

Internal Security Organisations of India

S.No.	Name of Organisation	Year of Creation	Headquarters
1.	Assam Rifles (A.R.)	1835	Shillong
2.	Central Reserve Police Force (C.R.P.F.)	1939	New Delhi
3.	Territorial Army	1948	In different States
4.	Indo-Tibetan Border Police	1962	New Delhi
5.	Home Guard	1962	In different States
6.	Coast Guard	1978	New Delhi
7.	Border Security Force (B.S.F.)	1965	New Delhi
8.	Central Industrial Security Force (C.I.S.F.)	1969	New Delhi
9.	National Security Guard	1984	New Delhi
10.	Police	—	In different States

Commander-in-Chiefs of India

1.	General Roy Bucher	Jan. 1, 1948 — Jan. 14, 1949
2.	General K. M. Kariappa	Jan. 15, 1949 — Jan. 14, 1953
3.	General Maharaj Rajendra Sinhji	Jan. 15, 1953 — March 31, 1955
4.	First Marshal of the Indian Air Force	Arjan Singh

First Chiefs of Staff of Indian Forces

1.	General Maharaj Rajendra Sinhji (Army Staff)	April 1, 1955 — May 14, 1955
2.	Vice Admiral R D. Katari (Naval Staff)	April 22, 1958 — June 4, 1962
3.	Air Marshal Sri Thomas Elmherst (Air Staff)	Aug. 15, 1947 — Feb. 21, 1950

Army Institutes

1.	Sainik Schools upto +2 Level	18 places in India
2.	Rashtriya Indian Military College (prepare for entrance to N.D.A)	Dehradun
3.	National Defence Academy (three services)	Khadakwasla, Pune
4.	Indian Military Academy (Army)	Dehradun
5.	Officers Training Academy (3 services) Short Courses	Chennai
6.	National Defence College	New Delhi
7.	The College of Combat	Mhow
8.	The College of Military Engineering	Kirkee
9.	Military College of Telecommunication Engineering	Mhow
10.	The armoured Corps Centre and School	Ahmed Nagar
11.	The School Artillery	Deolali
12.	The Infantry School	Mhow and Belgaum
13.	College of Material Management	Jabalpur

Air Force Institutions

Air Force Academy	Hyderabad	The College of Air Warfare	Secunderabad
Helicopter Training School	Hakimpet	Air Force Administrative College	Coimbatore
Flying Instructors School	Tambaram, Chennai	Air Force Technical College	Jalahalli

Defence Production Units

1.	Bharat Dynamics Ltd.	Hyderabad
2.	Praga Tools	Hyderabad
3.	Mishra Dhatu Nigam	Hyderabad
4.	Bharat Electronics Ltd.	Bangaluru
5.	Bharat Earthmovers Ltd.	Bangaluru
6.	Heavy Vehicles Ltd.	Avadi, Chennai
7.	Garden Reach Ship Builders and Engineers Ltd.	Kolkata
8.	Mazagaon Dock	Mumbai
9.	Goa Shipyard	Marmugao
10.	Hindustan Shipyard Ltd.	Vishakhapatnam
11.	Hindustan Aeronautics Ltd.	Bangalore, Hyderabad, Nasik, Koraput, Kanpur, Lucknow

(R-1641) GK–2

Transport

Railways

Important Facts:

1. Indian Railways are the biggest national undertaking.
2. The first Indian railway train rolled on its 34 km track from Mumbai to Thane on April 16, 1853.
3. Indian Railway is the largest railway network in Asia and world's second largest (First America) under one management.
4. The Chittaranjan Locomotive works, first of its kind in the country, was established after independence on January 26, 1950 but now electric engines are manufactured here. First of all it manufactured steam engines.
5. The number of stations, till 31st March, 2017, is 7,349.
6. As on 31st March, 2017 the total length of Indian railways is 67,368 km.
7. Till 31st March, 2017 Indian railways have 11,461 locomotives, 53,453 passenger Coaches, 6,714 other passenger trains coaches and 2,77,987 wagons.
8. About 35.32% of the railways routes have been electrified.
9. Railway finance was separated since 1924-25 from the general revenue. It have been merged in general revenue in 2017-18.
10. The only oldest running engine is *Fairy Queen*.
11. The first electric train rolled on from Mumbai to Kurla on 3rd February, 1925.
12. Kolkata Metro Rail is the first underground rail.
13. Delhi Metro Railways started on 24th December, 2002.
14. The longest railway journey which takes 82.30 hours from Dibrugarh to Kanyakumari (4,286 km).
15. The longest railway platform of the world is Gorakhpur (India). Its length is 1355.4 mt.
16. The longest tunnel of Indian railways between Banihal and Qazigund stations in J&K is 11.21 km long.
17. Indian Railway Board was established in 1905.
18. Indian Railways have three gauges—Broad gauge, metre gauge and narrow gauge.
19. In railways, there are A.C., first class and second class. Third class was removed in 1974.
20. Computer reservation facility, covering the 95% of the passenger population, is available at over 300 locations in the country.
21. Nehru Setu is the longest railway bridge built on river Sone.

Zones and Headquarters of Indian Railways

S. No.	Zone	Headquarters	S. No.	Zone	Headquarters
1.	Central	Mumbai (Victoria Terminus)	10.	East Coast	Bhubaneswar
2.	Eastern	Kolkata	11.	East Central	Hajipur
3.	Northern	New Delhi	12.	North Central	Allahabad
4.	North-Eastern	Gorakhpur	13.	North Western	Jaipur
5.	North-East Frontier	Maligaon, Guwahati	14.	South Western	Bangaluru (Hubli)
6.	Southern	Chennai	15.	West Central	Jabalpur
7.	South-Central	Secunderabad	16.	South East Central	Bilaspur
8.	South-Eastern	Kolkata	17.	Kolkata Metro Railway	Kolkata
9.	Western	Mumbai, Churchgate			

Road Transport

Important Facts:

1. The road network in India is one of the largest in the world.
2. The total length of roads, at present is 56.17 lakh km.
3. The total length of National Highways is 1,29,709 km including State Highways and other roads.
4. The Central Government owns the responsibility of 1,29,709 km long national highways.
5. Border Road Organisation was established in 1960.
6. Though the national highways do not constitute even 2 per cent of the total road length of the country, they bear about 40% of the traffic.
7. In our country, Maharashtra has the highest length of roads whereas the lowest length of road has Lakshadweep.
8. National Highways Development Project has been launched to link the four corners of the country by four or six lanes in a network. The four major cities—Kolkata, Delhi, Chennai and Mumbai will be linked by 5,882 km long roads in golden quadrilateral.
9. Indian roads have been divided into three parts—(a) National Highways (b) State Highways (c) Border Roads.
10. NH44 is the longest and NH47A is the smallest highway of India.

Shipping

Important Facts:

1. India has 7,516 km long coast line.
2. India has the largest merchant shipping fleet among the developing countries and ranks 17th in the world in shipping tonnage.
3. Cochin Shipyard Ltd., Kochi is the largest shipyard in the country.
4. Mumbai is the biggest port in the country. It is a natural harbour and handles more than one-fifth of the total traffic of the ports.
5. The public sector company, The Shipping Corporation of India Limited was established on 2nd October, 1961.
6. There are 13 major ports in the country apart from about 200 minor ports. Major ports are under Central Government and others are maintained by State Governments.

Major Ports of the Country: 1. Kolkata, 2. Mumbai, 3. Nhava Sheva (J.L. Nehru Port), 4. Tuticorin, 5. Chennai, 6. Mormugao, 7. New Mangalore, 8. Paradeep, 9. Kandla, 10. Vishakhapatnam, 11. Cochin, 12. Haldia, 13. Ennore.

Civil Aviation

Air India: Consequent upon merger of erstwhile Air India Ltd. and Indian Airlines, a new company viz., National Aviation Company of the India Limited (NACIL) was incorporated. Consequently post merger, the new entity is known as "Air India" and the appointed date of the merger is 1 April 2007. The "Maharaja" is retained as its mascot. The Registered Office of the Company is in New Delhi. Air India Ltd. is basically a passenger orientated airlines operating to 72 online domestic stations (including Alliance Air) and 42 international destinations in 28 countries. It is in transport services sector under the administrative control of the Ministry of Civil Aviation.

Major International Airports : Delhi (Indira Gandhi International Airport), Mumbai (Santacruz/Sahar), Kolkata (Dum Dum), Chennai (Meenambakkam), Amritsar (Raja Sansi) and Trivandrum (Thiruvananthapuram).

Indian Constitution & Polity

Indian Constitution is a comprehensive document and it is the lengthiest written Constitution in the World.

The Preamble of the Consti-tution: "We the people of India, having solemnly resolved to Constitute India into a Sovereign, Socialist, Secular Democratic Republic and to secure to all its citizen."

Justice: Social, economic and political.

Liberty: Of thought, expression, belief, faith and worship.

Equality: Of status and of opportunity, and to promote among them all.

Fraternity: Assuring the dignity of the individual and the unity and integrity of the nation.

In our constituent Assembly, this twenty-sixth day of November, 1949, do hereby adopt, enact and give to ourselves this constitution.

Schedules to the Constitution

The Constitution of India originally contained only eight schedules. Presently there are 12 schedules in the constitution.

First Schedule: It consists the list of the States and Union territories. *Second Schedule:* This Schedule is related to salary and allowances of the President, Governors, Speaker, Supreme Court and High Court Judges etc. *Third Schedule:* Contains forms of oath and affirmation. *Fourth Schedule:* Contains allocation of seats to each State and Union territory in the Council of States. *Fifth Schedule:* Provides for administration and control of scheduled areas and scheduled tribes. *Sixth Schedule:* Provides for administration of Tribal Areas in Assam, Meghalaya and Mizoram. *Seventh Schedule:* Distribution of powers and functions between the centre and state governments under three lists. *Eighth Schedule:* The languages recognised by Parliament. *Ninth Schedule:* It contains laws passed by the Union or States which cannot be taken to courts. *Tenth Schedule:* Provisions as to disqualification on the ground of political defection. *Eleventh Schedule:* Provisions regarding powers, authority etc. of Panchayati Raj institutions. *Twelfth Schedule:* Provisions regarding powers, authority etc. of Municipalities etc.

Foreign Sources of Indian Constitution

Foreign Sources	Subject	Foreign Sources	Subject
Britain	Parliamentary system, collective responsibilities of Cabinet	Canada	Division of powers
		Ireland	Directive principles
America	Fundamental right, Citizenship, Independent Judiciary, Judicial review	Germany	Emergency provisions
		Russia	Fundamental duties
		Australia	Concurrent list

The Supreme Court

Supreme Court of India, the highest Court of the country, consists of a Chief Justice and not more than 30 Judges appointed by the President. The Judges hold office till the age of 65. For appointment as a Judge of the Supreme Court, a person must be a citizen of India and must have been for at least five years as Judge of a High Court or Advocate of a High Court for at least ten years or he must be, in the opinion of the President, a distinguished jurist. The Supreme Court normally sits in New Delhi.

Chief Justices of India

S.No.	Name	Tenure
1.	Harilal J. Kania	Jan. 26, 1950 – Nov. 6, 1951
2.	M. Patanjali Sastri	Nov. 7, 1951 – Jan. 3, 1954
3.	Mehar Chand Mahajan	Jan. 4, 1954 – Dec. 22, 1954
4.	B.K. Mukherjee	Dec. 23, 1954 – Jan. 31, 1956
5.	S.R. Das	Feb. 1, 1956 – Sept. 30, 1959
6.	Bhuvaneshwar Prasad Sinha	Oct. 1, 1959, – Jan. 31, 1964
7.	P.B. Gajendragadkar	Feb. 1, 1964 – March 15, 1966
8.	A.K. Sarkar	March 16, 1966 – June 29, 1966
9.	K. Subba Rao	June 30, 1966 – April 11, 1967
10.	K. N. Wanchoo	April 12, 1967 – Feb. 24, 1968
11.	M. Hidayatullah	Feb. 25, 1968 – Dec. 16, 1970
12.	J.C. Shah	Dec. 17, 1970 – Jan. 21, 1971
13.	S.M. Sikri	Jan. 22, 1971 – April 25, 1973
14.	A.N. Roy	April 26, 1973 – January 27, 1977
15.	M.H. Beg	Jan. 28, 1977 – February 21, 1978
16.	Y.V. Chandrachud	Feb. 22, 1978 – July 11, 1985
17.	Prafullachandra Natvarlal Bhagwati	July 12, 1985 – Dec. 20, 1986
18.	R.S. Pathak	Dec. 21, 1986 – June 18, 1989
19.	E.S. Venkataramiah	June 19, 1989 – Dec. 18, 1989
20.	Sabyasachi Mukherjee	Dec. 19, 1989 – Sept. 25, 1990
21.	Ranganath Mishra	Sept. 26, 1990 – Nov. 24, 1991
22.	Kamal Narain Singh	Nov. 25, 1991 – Dec. 12, 1991
23.	M.H. Kania	Dec. 13, 1991 – Nov. 17, 1992
24.	Lalit Mohan Sharma	Nov. 18, 1992 – Feb. 11, 1993
25.	M.N. Venkatachaliah	Feb. 12, 1993 – Oct. 24, 1994
26.	Aziz Mushabber Ahmadi	Oct. 25, 1994 – March 24, 1997
27.	Jagdish Sharan Verma	March 25, 1997 – Jan. 17, 1998
28.	M.M. Punchhi	Jan. 18, 1998 – October 9, 1998
29.	A.S. Anand	Oct. 10, 1998 – Oct. 31, 2001
30.	S.P. Bharucha	Nov. 1, 2001 – May 4, 2002
31.	B.N. Kirpal	May 5, 2002 – Nov. 7, 2002
32.	G.B. Pattanaik	Nov. 8, 2002 – Dec. 18, 2002
33.	V.N. Khare	Dec. 19, 2002 – May 1, 2004
34.	S. Rajendra Babu	May 2, 2004 – June 1, 2004
35.	R.C. Lahoti	June 2, 2004 – Oct. 31, 2005
36.	Yogesh Kumar Sabharwal	Nov. 1, 2005 – Jan. 13, 2007
37.	K.G. Balakrishnan	Jan. 14, 2007 – May 11, 2010
38.	S.H. Kapadia	May 12, 2010 – Sept. 28, 2012
39.	Altamas Kabir	Sept. 29, 2012 – July 18, 2013
40.	P. Sadashivam	July 19, 2013 – April 26, 2014
41.	R.M. Lodha	April 27, 2014 – September 27, 2014
42.	H.L. Dattu	September 28, 2014 – Dec. 2, 2015
43.	T.S. Thakur	December 3, 2015 – January 3, 2017
44.	J.S. Khehar	January 4, 2017 – August 27, 2017
45.	Dipak Mishra	August 28, 2017 – October 2, 2018
46.	Ranjan Gogoi	October 3, 2018 – -------

Parliament

Parliament is the national legislature of the Indian Union. It consists of two Houses known as the Council of States or the Rajya Sabha and the House of People or Lok Sabha. The President is an integal part of Parliament.

Rajya Sabha: The Rajya Sabha is the Upper House of the Parliament and it is constituted of representatives from the States or the Constituent units of the Indian Union. It is a permanent body, one third of its members retiring after every two years. Its maximum strength is 250. Out of these, twelve members are nominated by the President from well-known personalities in the realm of Science, Art, Literature and Social Service. Rest of 238 representatives of the States and Union Territories are elected.

Lok Sabha: The Lok Sabha whose life is five years, is the Lower House of Parliament and comprises of members directly elected by the people. The House of the people (Lok Sabha) at present consists of 545 members of these, 530 members are directly elected from the states and 13 from Union Territories while 2 are nominated by the President from Anglo-Indian community. The House of the People shall continue for five years (unless sooner dissolved) from the date of its meeting and no longer and the expiry of the said period of 5 years shall operate as dissolution of the House.

Parliamentary Committees: There are several Parliamentary Committees to assist the Parliament in its deliberations. These are appointed or elected by the respective Houses of Lok Sabha and Rajya Sabha on a motion made or are nominated by their presiding officers, i.e., the Speaker of Lok Sabha and the Chairman of Rajya Sabha respectively. Broadly, Parliamentary Committees are of two kinds–standing committees and ad-hoc committees. Among the Standing Committees, three are financial Committees: (i) Public Account Committee; (ii) Estimate Committee; (iii) Public undertaking Committee.

Ad-hoc Committees are appointed as the need arises and cease to exist when the work is over.

Speaker of Lok Sabha: Speaker is elected by the Lok Sabha from among its members. The Speaker will have the final power to maintain order within the House of the People and to interpret its rules of procedure. Speaker decides whether a bill is a money bill or a non-money bill.

Speakers of Lok Sabha and Their Tenure

Lok Sabha	Speaker	Tenure
First	Ganesh Vasudev Mawlankar	15th May 1952 – 27th February 1956
	M.A. Iyenger	8 March 1956 – 10 May 1957
Second	M.A. Iyenger	11 May 1957 – 16 April 1962
Third	Hukum Singh	17 April 1962 – 16 March 1967
Fourth	Neelam Sanjeeva Reddy	17 March 1967 – 19 July 1969
	Dr. Gurudayal Singh Dillo	8 August 1969 – 19 March 1971
Fifth	Dr. Gurudayal Singh Dillo	22 March 1971 – 1 December 1975
	Baliram Bhagat	5 January 1976 – 25 March 1977
Sixth	Neelam Sanjeeva Reddy	26 March 1977 – 3 July 1977
	K.S. Hegde	21 July 1977 – 21 January 1980
Seventh	Dr. Balram Jakhar	22 January 1980 – 15 January 1985
Eighth	Dr. Balram Jakhar	16 January 1985 – 18 December 1989
Ninth	Ravi Rai	19 Dec 1989 – 10 July 1991
Tenth	Shivaraj V. Patil	10 July 1991 – 22 May 1996
Eleventh	P.A. Sangama	23 May 1996 – 23 March 1998
Twelfth	G.M.C. Balyogi	24 March 1998 – 21 October 1999
Thirteenth	G.M.C. Balyogi	27 Ocbober 1999 – 2 March 2002
	Nayeem Siddiqui (Acting)	3 March 2002 – 12 March 2002
	Manohar Joshi	12 May 2002 – 3 June 2004
Fourteenth	Somnath Chaterji	4 June 2004 – 2 June 2009
Fifteenth	Meira Kumar	3 June 2009 – 5 June 2014
Sixteenth	Sumitra Mahajan	6 June 2014 – 18 June 2019
Seventeenth	Om Birla	19 June 2019 – ------

Indian States: Allocation of Seats

S. No.	State	Seats of Lok Sabha	Seats of Rajya Sabha	Legislative Assembly	Legislative Council
1.	Andhra Pradesh	25	11	175	58
2.	Arunachal Pradesh	2	1	60	
3.	Assam	14	7	126	
4.	Bihar	40	16	243	75
5.	Chhattisgarh	11	5	90	
6.	Goa	2	1	40	
7.	Gujarat	26	11	182	
8.	Haryana	10	5	90	
9.	Himachal Pradesh	4	3	68	
10.	Jharkhand	14	6	81	
11.	Karnataka	28	12	224	75
12.	Kerala	20	9	140	
13.	Madhya Pradesh	29	11	230	
14.	Maharashtra	48	19	288	78
15.	Manipur	2	1	60	
16.	Meghalaya	2	1	60	
17.	Mizoram	1	1	40	
18.	Nagaland	1	1	60	
19.	Odisha	21	10	147	
20.	Punjab	13	7	117	
21.	Rajasthan	25	10	200	
22.	Sikkim	1	1	32	
23.	Tamil Nadu	39	18	234	
24.	Telangana	17	7	119	40
25.	Tripura	2	1	60	
26.	Uttar Pradesh	80	31	403	100
27.	Uttarakhand	5	3	70	
28.	West Bengal	42	16	295	

Union Territories

S. No.	U.T.	Seats of Lok Sabha	Seats of Rajya Sabha	Legislative Assembly	Legislative Council
1.	Andaman & Nicobar Islands	1	—	—	—
2.	Chandigarh	1	—	—	—
3.	Dadra and Nagar Haveli	1	—	—	—
4.	Daman and Diu	1	—	—	—
5.	Delhi	7	3	70	—
6.	Lakshadweep	1	—	—	—
7.	Puduchery	1	1	30	—
8.	Jammu & Kashmir*	6	4	87	36
9.	Ladakh	—	—	—	—

* Data of Ladakh is included in it.

Table of Precedence

1. President
2. Vice-President
3. Prime Minister
4. Governors of States within their respective states

5. Former Presidents
5A. Deputy Prime Minister
6. Chief Justice of India, Speaker of Lok Sabha
7. Cabinet Ministers of the Union, Chief Ministers of States within their respective States Deputy Chairman NITI Aayog. Former Prime Minister
Leaders of opposition in Rajya Sabha and Lok Sabha
7A. Holders of the Bharat Ratna Decoration
8. Ambassadors Extraordinary and Plenipotentiary and High Commissioners of Commonwealth Countries accredited to India.
Chief Ministers of States outside their respective States, Governors of states outside their respective states.
9. Judges of the Supreme Court
9A. Chairman of U.P.S.C., Chief Election Commissioner, Comptroller & Auditor General of India (CAG).
10. Deputy Chairman Rajya Sabha, Deputy Chief Minister of States, Deputy Speaker Lok Sabha, Members of the NITI Aayog, Minister of State of the Union and Other Minister in the Ministry of Defence.

President

The President is the Constitutional head of the Republic of India. He is more or less the titular head of the executive. Really speaking, he is the constitutional head but not the real executive. The real power is vested in the hands of the Council of Ministers.

Qualifications: (i) Indian citizen, (ii) age not less than 35 years, (iii) should have qualification for election to Lok Sabha, (iv) should not hold any office of profit, (v) should not be a Member of Parliament or State Legislature.

Powers: He makes appointments to all the constitutional posts. He can address either House of Parliament and dissolve Lok Sabha. All Bills passed by Parliament must receive his assent to become an Act. He issues ordinances when Parliament is not in session. No Money Bill can be introduced in Lok Sabha without his recommendation. He can grant pardon, reprieve or remit punishment and he can commute death sentences, can declare national emergency, state emergency and financial emergency.

Term and Emolument: The President holds the office for a period of five years. He is eligible for re-election. He draws the salary of ₹ 5.0 lakh per month with various allowances. He is also entitled to rent free official residence called Rashtrapati Bhawan.

PRESIDENTS OF INDIA

Dr. Rajendra Prasad	26 Jan., 1950—13 May, 1962
Dr. S. Radhakrishnan	13 May, 1962—13 May, 1967
Dr. Zakir Hussain	13 May, 1967—3 May, 1969
V.V. Giri (Acting)	3 May, 1969—20 July 1969
M. Hidayatullah (Acting)	20 July, 1969—24 Augt, 1969
V.V. Giri	24 Augt, 1969—24 Augt, 1974
Fakhruddin Ali Ahmed	24 Augt, 1974—11 Feb., 1977
B.D. Jatti (Acting)	11 Feb., 1977—25 July, 1977
Neelam Sanjeeva Reddy	25 July, 1977—25 July, 1982
Giani Zail Singh	25 July, 1982—25 July, 1987
R. Venktaraman	25 July, 1987—25 July, 1992
Dr. Shankar Dayal Sharma	25 July, 1992—25 July, 1997
K.R. Narayanan	25 July, 1997—25 July, 2002
A.P.J. Abdul Kalam	25 July, 2002—25 July, 2007
Pratibha Patil	25 July, 2007-25 July, 2012
Pranab Mukherjee	25 July, 2012-25 July, 2017
Ram Nath Kovind	25 July, 2017-...........

Vice-President

The Vice-President acts as the ex-officio Chairman of the Council of States (Rajya Sabha). He is elected by an electoral college consisting of the members of both Houses of Parliament in accordance with the system of proportional representation by means of the single transferable vote. He must be a citizen of India, not less than 35 years of age, and should be eligible for election as a member of the Council of States. Disputes in connection with election of a president or a vice-president are to be a dealt with in accordance with Article-71. Such disputes shall be decided by the Supreme Court.

General Knowledge

Prime Minister

The Constitution lays down that there shall be a Council of Ministers headed by the Prime Minister to aid and advise the President in the exercise of his functions.

The Prime Minister is the head of the Cabinet. Other Ministers are appointed by the President on his advice. He is the leader of the majority party in the Lok Sabha.

PRIME MINISTERS OF INDIA		
Jawahar Lal Nehru	August 15, 1947	— May 27, 1964
Gulzari Lal Nanda (Acting)	May 27, 1964	— June 9, 1964
Lal Bahadur Shastri	June 9, 1964	— January 11, 1966
Gulzari Lal Nanda (Acting)	January 11, 1966	— January 24, 1966
Indira Gandhi	January 24, 1966	— March 24, 1977
Morarji Desai	March 24, 1977	— July 28, 1979
Charan Singh	July 28, 1979	— January 14, 1980
Indira Gandhi	January 14, 1980	— October 31, 1984
Rajiv Gandhi	October 31, 1984	— December 1, 1989
Vishwanath Pratap Singh	December 18, 1989	— November 10, 1990
Chandrashekhar	November 10, 1990	— June 21, 1991
P.V. Narasimha Rao	June 21, 1991	— May 15, 1996
Atal Behari Bajpayee	May 15, 1996	— June 1, 1996
H.D. Deve Gowda	June 1, 1996	— April 21, 1997
I.K. Gujral	April 21, 1997	— March 19, 1998
Atal Behari Bajpayee	March 19, 1998	— May 22, 2004
Dr. Manmohan Singh	May 22, 2004	— May 26, 2014
Narendra Modi	May 26, 2014	— ....

Fundamental Rights

Following fundamental rights are enjoyed by every Indian citizen, irrespective of caste, colour, creed and sex:

1. **Right to Equality:** No special privileges, no distinction on grounds of religion, caste, creed and sex.

2. **Right to Freedom:** The right to freedom of expression and speech, the right to choose one's own profession, the right to reside in any part of the Indian Union.

3. **Right to Freedom to Religion:** Except when it is in the interest of public order, morality, health or other conditions, everybody has the right to profess, practice and propagate his religion freely.

4. **Cultural and Educational Rights:** The Constitution provides that every community can run its own institutions to preserve its own culture and language.

5. **Right against Exploitation:** Traffic in human beings and forced labour and the employment of children under 14 years in factories or mines, are punishable offences.

6. **Rights to Constitutional Remedies:** When a citizen finds that any of his fundamental rights has been encroached upon, he can move the Supreme Court, which has been empowered to safeguard the fundamental rights of a citizen (Article 32).

Jurisdiction and Seat of High Courts

Name	Year	Territorial Jurisdiction	Seat
Allahabad	1866	Uttar Pradesh	Allahabad (Bench at Lucknow)
Andhra Pradesh#	2019	Andhra Pradesh	Amaravati
Bombay	1862	Maharashtra, Goa, Dadar and Nagar Haveli and Daman and Diu	Mumbai (Benches at Nagpur, Panaji and Aurangabad)
Calcutta	1862	West Bengal and Andaman & Nicobar	Kolkata (Circuit Bench at Port Blair)
Chhattisgarh	2000	Chhattisgarh	Bilaspur
Delhi	1966	Delhi	Delhi
Guwahati	1948	Assam, Nagaland, Mizoram and Arunachal Pradesh	Guwahati (Benches at Kohima, Aizawl and Itanagar)
Gujarat	1960	Gujarat	Ahmedabad
Himachal Pradesh	1971	Himachal Pradesh	Shimla
Jammu & Kashmir	1928	Jammu & Kashmir	Srinagar and Jammu
Jharkhand	2000	Jharkhand	Ranchi
Karnataka	1884	Karnataka	Bengaluru (Circuit Benches at Dharwar and Gulbarga)
Kerala	1958	Kerala & Lakshadweep	Ernakulam
Madhya Pradesh	1956	Madhya Pradesh	Jabalpur (Benches at Gwalior & Indore)
Madras	1862	Tamil Nadu & Puducherry	Chennai (Bench at Madurai)
Orissa	1948	Odisha	Cuttack
Patna	1916	Bihar	Patna
Punjab and Haryana	1966	Punjab, Haryana and Chandigarh	Chandigarh
Rajasthan	1949	Rajasthan	Jodhpur (Bench at Jaipur)
Sikkim	1975	Sikkim	Gangtok
Uttarakhand	2000	Uttarakhand	Nainital
Tripura	2013	Tripura	Agartala
Meghalaya	2013	Meghalaya	Shillong
Manipur	2013	Manipur	Imphal
Telangana*	2019	Telangana	Hyderabad

High court of Andhra Pradesh to function at Amaravati from January 1, 2019.

* Originally known as Andhra Pradesh High Court and it was established on 5 November 1956 but it was renamed as High Court of Judicature at Hyderabad in 2014, renamed again as Telangana high Court on 1 January 2019.

Fundamental Duties

The fundamental duties for the Indian citizens have been incorporated in the Constitution through the Constitution (42nd) Amendment Act, 1976. These duties are: **(i)** to abide by the Constitution and respect its ideals and institutions, the National Flag and the National Anthem; **(ii)** to cherish and follow the noble deeds which inspired our national struggle for freedom; **(iii)** to uphold and protect the sovereignty, unity and integrity of India; **(iv)** to defend the country and render national service when called upon to do so; **(v)** to promote harmony and the spirit of common brotherhood amongst all the people transcending religious, regional or sectional diversities and to renounce practices derogatory to the dignity of women; **(vi)** to value and preserve the rich heritage of our composite culture; **(vii)** to protect and improve natural environment including forests, lakes, rivers and wildlife, and to have compassion for living creatures; **(viii)** to develop the scientific temper, humanism and the spirit of inquiry and reform; **(ix)** to safeguard public property and to abjure violence; **(x)** to strive towards excellence in all spheres of individual and collective activity so that the nation constantly rises to higher levels of endeavour and achievement. **(xi)** who is parent or guardian to provide opportunities for education to his child or, as the case may be, ward between age of six and fourteen years.

Directive Principles of State Policy

The Directive Principles of State Policy are contained in Article 36 to 51 in Part IV of the constitutions. Directive principles are not enforceable through courts. Main aim of Directive principles is to provide social and economic base of a genuine democracy.

Some Important Directive Principles:
- Provisions for adequate means of livelihood for all citizens (Art. 39).
- Right to work (Art. 41).
- Right to human condition of work and maternity relief (Art. 42).
- Right to a living wage and condition of work ensuring decent standard of life of worker (Art. 43).
- Common Civil Code (Art. 44).
- Prohibit consumption of liquor (Art. 47).
- Prevent slaughter of useful cattle (Art. 48).
- Organise Panchayati Raj (Art. 40).
- Separate the judiciary from the executive (Art. 50).
- Protect and maintain places of historic monuments (Art. 49).
- International peace (Art. 51).

Voting Age: The voting age in the election to the Lok Sabha and State Legislative Assemblies has been reduced from 21 to 18 years by the Constitution (61st) Amendment Act, 1989.

Governor

The Governor is appointed by the President and holds office during the pleasure of the President. Apart from the power to appoint the council of ministers, if the governor finds that the government of state cannot be carried on in accordance with the provisions of the constitution (Art. 356), he may send his report to the President who may assume to himself the functions of the government of the state. (This is popularly known as 'President's Rule').

The Attorney General of India

The Attorney General of India is the first law officer of the Government of India. Though he is not a member of cabinet he has the right to speak in the House of Parliament, but he has no right to vote. The Attorney General of India shall be appointed by the President and shall hold office during his pleasure. His duty shall be to give advice on such legal matter from time to time as may be referred to him by the President.

Comptroller & Auditor General of India (CAG)

The Comptroller and Auditor General of India is guardian of the public purse and it is his duty to see that not a *paisa* is spent out of consolidated fund of India or of a state without the authority of the appropriate legislature. He is appointed by President of India.

Status
- Appointed by the President.
- A person with long administrative experience & knowledge of accounts is appointed.

- Holds office for 6 yrs or till 65 yrs of age.
- The President can remove him only on the recommendation of the 2 houses of Parliament (as in case of judge of Supreme Court).

Inter-State Councils

Article 263 provides for inter-state councils. The power of the President to set up Inter-State Councils not only for advising upon disputes but also for investigating and discussing subjects in which some or all of the states, or the Union and one or more of the states have common interest.

Union Public Service Commission (U.P.S.C.)

This Commission is responsible for (i) recruitment to all civil services and posts, under the Union Government by written examinations, interviews and promotions, and (ii) advising the Government on all matters relating to methods of recruitment, principles to be followed in making promotions and transfers. Its Chairman is appointed by the President.

Staff Selection Commission

The Union Government has constituted the Staff Selection Commission for recruitment to non-technical Group C and some of Group B posts in the central departments and in subordinate offices. The administrative Reforms Commission had recommended the setting up of such a Commission.

Chief Election Commissioners of India

S.No.	Name	Tenure
1.	Sukumar Sen	21 March, 1950 – 19 Dec., 1958
2.	K.V.K. Sundaram	20 Dec., 1958 – 30 Sept., 1967
3.	S.P. Sen Verma	1 Oct., 1967 – 30 Sept., 1972
4.	Dr. Nagendra Singh	1 Oct., 1972 – 6 Feb., 1973
5.	T. Swaminathan	7 Feb., 1973 – 17 June, 1977
6.	S.L. Shakdhar	18 June, 1977 – 17 June, 1982
7.	R.K. Trivedi	18 June, 1982 – 31 Dec., 1985
8.	R.V.S. Peri Sastri	1 Jan., 1986 – 25 Nov., 1990
9.	Smt. V.S. Rama Devi	26 Nov., 1990 – 11 Dec., 1990
10.	T.N. Sheshan	12 Dec., 1990 – 11 Dec., 1996
11.	M.S. Gill	12 Dec., 1996 – 13 June, 2001
12.	J.M. Lyngdoh	13 June 2001 – 6 Feb., 2004
13.	T.S. Krishnamurthy	7 Feb., 2004 – 15 May, 2005
14.	B.B. Tandan	15 May, 2005 –29 June, 2006
15.	N. Gopalaswami	30 June, 2006 – 20 April, 2009
16.	Navin Chawla	21 April, 2009 – 29 July, 2010
17.	S.Y. Quraishi	30 July, 2010 – 10 June, 2012
18.	V.S. Sampath	11 June, 2012 – 15 Jan., 2015
19.	Harishankar Brahma	16 Jan., 2015 – 18 April, 2015
20.	Nasim Zaidi	19 April, 2015 – 5 July, 2017
21.	Achal Kumar Jyoti	6 July, 2017 – 22 Jan., 2018
22.	Om Prakash Rawat	23 Jan., 2018 – 01 Dec., 2018
23.	Sunil Arora	02 December, 2018 – —

Planning In India

The need for planning was felt in India even before independence. A National Planning Committee was set up by the Indian National Congress as early as 1938. The Planning Commission was set up in 1950. It was an advisory body engaged in the task of meaningful national planning. The main objectives of India's Economic Planning are as follows : (i) securing an increase in National Income; (ii) achieving a planned rate of investment within a given period to bring the actual investment as a proportion of national income to a higher level; (iii) reducing inequality in the distribution of income and wealth; (iv) providing additional employment; (v) adopting measures to increase agricultural production, manufacturing capacity for producers and a favourable balance of payments.

Five Year Plans in India

Plans	Period	Investment (Rs. Crore)	Objectives
First Plan	April 1, 1951-March 31, 1956	1,960	Priority to agriculture, electricity and irrigation.
Second Plan	April 1, 1956—March 31, 1961	4,672	Development of basic and heavy industries.
Third Plan	April 1, 1961—March 31, 1966	8,577	Long term development of India's economy.
Annual Plan	April 1, 1966—March 31, 1967	2,137	
Annual Plan	April 1, 1967—March 31, 1968	2,205	
Annual Plan	April 1,1968—March 31, 1969	2,283	
Fourth Plan	April 1, 1969—March 31, 1974	15,779	Enlarge the income of rural population and supply of goods of mass consumption.
Fifth Plan	April 1,1974—March 31, 1979	39,426	Attain increased self reliance and employment avenues.
Annual Plan	April 1, 1979—March 31, 1980	12,176	
Sixth Plan	April 1, 1980—March 31, 1985	1,09,292	Removal of unemployment
Seventh Plan	April 1, 1985—March 31, 1990	2,18,730	Food work and productivity were the basic priorities.
Eighth Plan	April, 1992—March 31, 1997	4,95,670	Raising employment
Ninth Plan	April 1, 1997—March 31, 2002	9,41,041	Agriculture and rural development
Tenth Plan	April 1, 2002—March 31, 2007	14,91,610	Growth rate 7.8 percent per annum.
Eleventh Plan	April 1, 2007—March 31, 2012	36,44,718	Literacy, Employment, Rural development & Transport development.
Twelfth Plan	April 1, 2012–March 31, 2017	76,69,807	Long term development of India's economy.

15-Year Vision Plan

With the end of the Twelfth Plan in March 2017 the era of five year plans came to an end. NITI Aayog has come forward with a draft 15-year vision plan to catapult the country's economy to more than three times as compared to the present day. The new plan is set to replace the centralised five-year plans the country has been following for decades. The new plan is accompanied by shorter sub-plans—a seven-year strategy for 2017-24, and a three-year 'Action Agenda' from 2017-18 to 2019-20. No less than 300 specific action points covering a wide range of sectors have been drawn up as part of the 15-year vision. The 15-year vision document has a seven-year strategy document for 2017-24 as the 'National Development Agenda'. Separately, a three-year 'Action Agenda' from 2017-18 to 2019-20 is also under works to assess funding requirements. The three-year agenda is further divided into seven parts, with a number of specific action points for each part to boost economic growth. India's urban population is expected to increase by 22 crores by 2031. The plan is likely to lay emphasis on urban development, taking a note from China's elaborate long-term development agenda.

NITI Aayog

The government on January 1, 2015 replaced the 65-year-old Planning Commission—a relic of the Socialist era—with a NITI Aayog or National Institution for Transforming India, marking a major shift in policy making by involving states. The Aayog will recommend a national agenda, including strategic and technical advice on elements of policy and economic matters. It will also develop mechanisms for village-level plans and aggregate these progressively at higher levels of government.

Finance Commission

Article 280 of the Constitution provides for the appointment of a finance commission every five year. President appoints chairman and members of this commission. Finance commission are to recommend to President the basis for the distribution of the net proceeds of taxes between the centre and the states and the principles which should govern the grants-in-aid to be given to the states out of the consolidated funds of India.

Finance Commission of India

S. No.	Year of Constitution	Name of Commissioner	Years of Execution
1st	1951	K.C. Niyogi	1952 – 1957
2nd	1956	K. Santhanam	1957 – 1962
3rd	1960	A.K. Chanda	1962 – 1966
4th	1964	Dr. P.V. Rajamannar	1966 – 1969
5th	1968	Mahavir Tyagi	1969 – 1974
6th	1972	Brahmanand Reddy	1974 – 1979
7th	1977	J.M. Shallot	1979 – 1984
8th	1983	Y.V. Chavan	1984 – 1989
9th	1987	Dr. K.P. Salve	1989 – 1995
10th	1992	K.C. Pant	1995 – 2000
11th	1998	A.M. Khusro	2000 – 2005
12th	2002	Dr. C. Rangrajan	2005 – 2010
13th	2007	Dr. V.L. Kelkar	2010 – 2015
14th	2013	Y.V. Reddy	2015 – 2020
15th	2017	N.K. Singh	2020 – 2025

National Development Council

The National Development Council, set-up in 1952, consists of representatives of the Central Government as well as the State governments. It is the supreme body insofar as planning is concerned and it determines policies, issues guidelines, reviews working of the plan and finally approves the plan. The Council consists of the Prime Minister (Chairman), all Union Cabinet Ministers, Chief Ministers of all States and Union Territories and the Vice Chairman and members of the NITI Aayog. For matters relating to Plans and Planning, the Union Minister of Planning is responsible to the Parliament.

Stock Exchange

1. Mumbai	2. Chennai	3. Coimbtore	4. Kolkata
5. New Delhi	6. Ahmedabad	7. Vadodara	8. Rajkot
9. Kutch	10. Hyderabad	11. Bengaluru	12. Mangalore
13. Hubli-Dharwar	14. Kochi	15. Bhubaneshwar	16. Jaipur
17. Indore	18. Kanpur	19. Ludhiana	20. Guwahati
21. Magadh (Patna)	22. Pune		

Reserve Bank of India

- It is the Central Bank of the country.
- It was established on April 1, 1935 with a capital of ₹ 5 crore. This capital of ₹ 5 crore was divided into 5 lakh equity shares of ₹ 100 each. In the beginning, the ownership of almost all the share capital was with the non-government share-holders.
- It was nationalized on Jan 1, 1949 as govt. acquired the private share-holdings.
- **Governors:** Ist Governor - Sir Smith (1935-37)
  Ist Indian Governor - C.D. Deshmukh (1948-49)

Other Financial Institutions

Industrial Credit & Investment Corporation of India Bank (ICICI Bank)	• Established in 1955 as a public limited company to encourage and assist industrial units of the nation. It has been converted into a bank with effect from May 3, 2002.
Small Industries Development Bank of India (SIDBI)	• Established in 1990; promotes small scale sector.
National Bank of Agriculture & Rural Development (NABARD)	• Established on Nov 5, 1982; gives credit facilities to farmers.
Export-Import Bank of India (EXIM)	• Set-up on Jan 1, 1982; grants deferred credit to Indian exporters in order to operate in the International market.
Industrial Development Bank of India (IDBI)	• Established in 1964; to provide financial assistance to industrial enterprises.
Industrial Reconstruction Bank of India (IRBI)	• Set-up in 1971 with the objective of reviving and revitalizing sick industrial units in public and private sectors.

INVENTIONS AND DISCOVERIES

IMPORTANT INVENTIONS

Name of Invention	Inventor	Nationality	Year
Aeroplane	Orville & Wilbur Wright	U.S.A.	1903
Ball-Point Pen	John J. Loud	U.S.A.	1888
Barometer	Evangelista Torricelli	Italy	1644
Bicycle	Kirkpatrick Macmillan	Britain	1839-40
Bifocal Lens	Benjamin Franklin	U.S.A.	1780
Car (Petrol)	Karl Benz	Germany	1888
Celluloid	Alexander Parkes	Britain	1861
Cinema	Nicolas & Jean Lumiere	France	1895
Clock (mechanical)	I-Hsing & Liang Ling-Tsan	China	725
Diesel Engine	Rudolf Diesel	Germany	1895
Dynamo	Hypolite Pixii	France	1832
Electric Lamp	Thomas Alva Edison	U.S.A.	1879
Electric Motor (DC)	Zenobe Gramme	Belgium	1873
Electric Motor (AC)	Nikola Tesla	U.S.A.	1888
Electro-magnet	William Sturgeon	Britain	1824
Electronic Computer	Dr. Alan M. Turing	Britain	1943
Film (moving outlines)	Louis Prince	France	1885
Film (musical sound)	Dr. Le de Forest	U.S.A.	1923
Fountain Pen	Lewis E. Waterman	U.S.A.	1884
Gramophone	Thomas Alva Edison	U.S.A.	1878
Helicopter	Etienne Oehmichen	France	1924
Jet Engine	Sir Frank Whittle	Britain	1937
Laser	Charles H. Townes	U.S.A.	1960
Lift (Mechanical)	Elisha G. Otis	U.S.A.	1852
Locomotive	Richard Trevithick	Britain	1804
Machine Gun	James Puckle	Britain	1718
Microphone	Alexander Graham Bell	U.S.A.	1876
Microscope	Z. Janssen	Netherlands	1590
Motor Cycle	G. Daimler	Germany	1885
Photography (on film)	John Carbutt	U.S.A.	1888
Printing Press	Johann Gutenberg	Germany	c.1455
Razor (safety)	King C. Gillette	U.S.A.	1895

Name of Invention	Inventor	Nationality	Year
Refrigerator	James Harrison & Alexander Catlin	U.S.A.	1850
Safety Pin	Walter Hunt	U.S.A.	1849
Sewing machine	Barthelemy Thimmonnier	France	1829
Ship (steam)	J.C. Perier	France	1775
Ship (turbine)	Hon. Sir C. Parsons	Britain	1894
Skyscraper	W. Le Baron Jenny	U.S.A.	1882
Slide Rule	William Oughtred	Britain	1621
Steam Engine (condenser)	James Watt	Britain	1765
Steel Production	Henry Bessemer	Britain	1855
Steel (stainless)	Harry Brearley	Britain	1913
Submarine	David Bushnell	U.S.A.	1776
Tank	Sir Ernest Swinton	Britain	1914
Telegraph	M. Lammond	France	1787
Telegraph Code	Samuel F.B. Morse	U.S.A.	1837
Telephone (perfected)	Alexander Graham Bell	U.S.A.	1876
Television (mechanical)	John Logie Baird	Britain	1926
Television (electronic)	P.T. Farnsworth	U.S.A.	1927
Thermometer	Galileo Galilei	Italy	1593
Transformer	Michael Faraday	Britain	1831
Transistor	Bardeen, Shockley & Brattain	U.S.A.	1948
Washing Machine (elec.)	Hurley Machine Co.	U.S.A.	1907
Zip-Fastener	W.L. Judson	U.S.A.	1891

Important Discoveries

Discovery	Discoverer	Nationality	Year
Aluminium	Hans Christian Oerstedt	Denmark	1827
Atomic number	Henry Moseley	England	1913
Atomic structure of matter	John Dalton	England	1803
Chlorine	C.W. Scheele	Sweden	1774
Electromagnetic induction	Michael Faraday	England	1831
Electromagnetic waves	Heinrich Hertz	Germany	1886
Electromagnetism	Hans Christian Oersted	Denmark	1920
Electron	Sir Joseph Thomson	England	1897
General theory of relativity	Albert Einstein	Switzerland	1915
Hydrogen	Henry Cavendish	England	1766
Law of electric conduction	Georg Ohm	Germany	1827
Law of electromagnetism	Andre Ampere	France	1826
Law of falling bodies	Galileo	Italy	1590
Laws of gravitation & motion	Isaac Newton	England	1687
Laws of planetary motion	Johannes Kepler	Germany	1609-10
Magnesium	Sir Humphry Davy	England	1808
Neptune (Planet)	Johann Galle	Germany	1846
Neutron	James Chadwick	England	1932
Nickel	Axel Cronstedt	Sweden	1751
Nitrogen	Daniel Rutherford	England	1772

Discovery	Discoverer	Nationality	Year
Oxygen	Joseph Priestly	England	1772
	C.W. Scheele	Sweden	
Ozone	Christian Schonbein	Germany	1839
Pluto (Planet)	Clyde Tombaugh	U.S.A	1930
Plutonium	G.T. Seaborg	U.S.A	1940
Proton	Ernest Rutherford	England	1919
Quantum Theory	Max Planck	Germany	1900
Radioactivity	Antoine Bacquerel	France	1896
Radium	Pierre & Marie Curie	France	1898
Silicon	Jons Berzelius	Sweden	1824
Special theory of relativity	Albert Einstein	Switzerland	1905
Sun as centre of solar system	Copernicus	Poland	1543
Uranium	Martin Klaproth	Germany	1789
Uranus (Planet)	William Herschel	England	1781
X-rays	Wilhelm Roentgen	Germany	1895

Geographical Explorations/Discoveries

Place	Explorer/Discoverer	Nationality	Year
America	Christopher Columbus	Italy	1492
Hawaii Islands (Sandwich Islands)	Captain James Cook	England	1778
Newfoundland	John Cabot	England	1497
New Zealand	Abel Janszoon Tasman	Holland	1642
North Pole	Robert Peary	USA	1909
Sea Route to India (via Cape of Good Hope)	Vasco da Gama	Portugal	1498
South Pole	Roald Amundsen	Norway	1911

Scientific Instruments

Name of Instrument	Used for
Altimeter	measuring altitude
Ammeter	measuring strength of an electric current
Anemometer	measuring the velocity of wind
Audiometer	measuring level of hearing
Barometer	measuring atmospheric pressure
Callipers	measuring the internal and external diameters of tubes
Calorimeter	measuring quantity of heat
Compass	finding out direction
Dynamo	converting mechanical energy into electrical energy
Eudiometer	measuring volume changes during chemical reactions between gases
Galvanometer	detecting and determining the strength of small electric currents
Hydrometer	measuring specific gravity of a liquid
Hygrometer	measuring the humidity in the atmosphere
Lactometer	measuring the purity of milk

Name of Instrument	Used for
Manometer	measuring the gaseous pressure
Micrometer	measuring minute distances, angles, etc.
Microscope	seeing magnified view of very small objects
Periscope	with the help of this instrument an observer in a submarine can see what is going on the surface of the sea
Photometer	measuring intensity of light from distant stars
Pyrometer	measuring high temperatures
Radar	detecting and finding the presence and location of moving objects like aircraft, missile, etc.
Radiometer	measuring the emission of radiant energy
Rain Gauge	measuring the amount of rainfall
Seismograph	measuring and recording the intensity and origin of earthquake shocks
Sextant	measuring altitude and angular distances between two objects or heavenly bodies
Spectrometer	measuring the refractive indices
Spherometer	measuring the curvature of spherical objects/surface
Sphygmomanometer	measuring blood pressure
Stethoscope	ascertaining the condition of heart and lungs by listening to their function
Stroboscope	viewing objects that are moving rapidly with a periodic motion as if they were at rest
Tachometer	measuring the rate of revolution or angular speed of a revolving shaft
Telescope	viewing magnified images of distant objects
Theodolite	measuring the horizontal and vertical angles
Thermocouple	measuring the temperature inside furnaces and jet engines
Thermometer	measuring human body temperature
Thermostat	regulating constant temperature
Ultrasonoscope	measuring utrasonic sounds
Viscometer	measuring the viscosity of a fluid
Voltmeter	measuring potential difference between two points.

DISEASES AND THE PARTS OF BODY THEY AFFECT

Disease	Part of body affected	Disease	Part of body affected
AIDS	Immune system of body	Jaundice	Liver
Arthritis	Inflammation of joints	Meningitis	Brain or spinal cord
Asthma	Lungs	Pleurisy	Pleura (inflammation of)
Cataract	Eyes	Polio	motor neurons
Conjunctivitis	Eyes	Pneumonia	Lungs
Diabetes	Pancreas	Pyorrhoea	Sockets of teeth
Diphtheria	Throat	Tuberculosis	Lungs
Glaucoma	Eyes	Typhoid	Intestine
Eczema	Skin	Malaria	Spleen
Goitre	Front of the neck (due to enlargement of thyroid gland)	Leukaemia	Blood
Gout	Joints of bone	Rickets	Bones

Space Research

First in Space

First creator of rules regarding space research	— Isaac Newton
First artificial satellite launched in space	— Sputnik-1 (1957)
First living being sent in space	— Louika (a dog)
Firstever manned spacecraft	— Vostok-I
First man in space	— Yuri Gagarin U.S.S.R. (1961)
First woman in space	— Valentina Tereshkova U.S.S.R. (June 1963)
First man who moved in space out of the spacecraft	— Alexi Livonov U.S.S.R. (June 1965)
First person to land on moon	— Neil Armstrong, America (21st July, 1969)
First fourwheeled carriage without human being on moon	— Leunokhev-I U.S.S.R. (1970)
First space lab in orbit	— Skylab (America, 1973)
First space shuttle	— Columbia (America, 1981)
First Indian (man) in space	— Squadron leader—Rakesh Sharma (13th April, 1984)
First Indian (Woman) in space	— Kalpana Chawla (19th Nov., 1997)
First American woman in space	— Sailyride (1983)
First spacecraft on Mars	— Pathfinder (6 July, 1997)
First woman who lead spacecraft	— Allin Collis (America)
First spacecraft without man	— Shenzoo, China (20th Nov. 1999)

Indian Space Programme : At a Glance

Satellite	Date	Type	Launch Vehicle	Result
Aryabhatta	19-04-75	Scientific	Cosmos	successful
Bhaskara I	07-06-79	Geosurvey	Cosmos	successful
Rohini	10-08-79	Geosurvey	S.L.V.3	unsuccessful
Rohini D-1	18-07-80	Geosurvey	S.L.V.3	successful
Rohini	31-05-81	Scientific	S.L.V.3	successful
Apple	19-06-81	Communication	Ariane	successful
Bhaskara II	20-11-81	Geosurvey	Cosonos	successful
INSAT-1A	10-04-82	Multipurpose	Delta	unsuccessful
Rohini	17-04-83	Scientific	S.L.V.3	successful
INSAT-1B	30-08-83	Multipurpose	Space Shuttle	successful
SROSS I	24-03-87	Technical	ASLV-D1	unsuccessful

Satellite	Date	Type	Launch Vehicle	Result
IRS-1A	17-03-88	Remote sensing	Vostok	successful
INSAT-1D	12-06-90	Multipurpose	Delta	successful
IRS-1B	29-08-91	Remote sensing	Vostok	successful
INSAT-2A	10-07-92	Multipurpose	Ariane	successful
SROSS-4	04-05-94	Scientific	ASLV-D3	successful
IRS-P2	15-10-94	Remote sensing	PSLV-D2	successful
INSAT-2C	07-12-95	Telecom	Ariane-4	successful
IRS-1C	28-12-95	Remote sensing	PSLV-D3	successful
IRS-P3	20-03-96	Remote sensing	PSLV-D3	successful
IRS-ID	29-09-97	Remote sensing	PSLV	successful
INSAT-2E	03-04-99	Multipurpose	Ariane	successful
INSAT-3B	22-03-2000	Multipurpose	Ariane	successful
G-SAT-1	18-04-2001	Multipurpose	GSLV-D	successful
INSAT-3C	24-01-2002	Communication	Ariane-4	successful
MAT SAT	12-09-2002	Meteorology	PSLVC-4	successful
INSAT-3A	10-04-2003	Multipurpose	Ariane-5	successful
INSAT-3E	28-09-2003	Communication	Ariane-5	successful
INSAT-4A	22-12-2005	Communication	Ariane-5	successful
CARTOSAT-2	10-01-2007	Communication	PSLV-C7	successful
INSAT-4B	12-03-2007	Communication	Ariane-5	successful
Chandrayaan-1	22-10-2008	Mapping and Scientific	PSLV-C11	successful
Oceansat-2	24-09-2009	Remote Sensing	PSLV-C14	successful
CARTOSAT-2B	12-07-2010	Communication	PSLV-C15	successful
RESOURCESAT-2	20-04-2011	Remote Sensing	PSLV-C16	successful
GSAT-12	15-07-2011	Communication	PSLV-C17	successful
Megha-Tropiques	12-10-2011	Mapping and Scientific	PSLV-C18	successful
RISAT-1	26-04-2012	Remote Sensing	PSLV-C19	successful
Spot-6	09-09-2012	Remote Sensing	PSLV-C21	successful
Saral	25-02-2013	Scientific	PSLV-C20	successful
GSAT-7	30-08-2013	Defence	Ariane-5	successful
Mangalyan	05-11-2013	Mapping and Scientific	PSLV-C25	successful
GSAT-14	05-01-2014	Communication	GSLV-D5	successful
IRNSS-1B	04-04-2014	Mapping and Scientific	PSLV-C24	successful
Spot-7	30-06-2014	Remote Sensing	PSLV-C23	successful
IRNSS-1C	16-10-2014	Mapping and Scientific	PSLV-C26	successful
IRNSS-1D	28-03-2015	Mapping and Scientific	PSLV-C27	successful
GSAT-6	27-08-2015	Communication	GSLV-D6	successful
Astrosat	28-09-2015	Mapping and Scientitic	PSLV-C30	successful
GSAT-15	11-11-2015	Communication	Ariane-5	successful
TELEOS-1	16-12-2015	Mapping and Scientific	PSLV-C29	successful
IRNSS-1E	20-01-2016	Mapping and Scientific	PSLV-C31	successful
IRNSS-1F	10-03-2016	Mapping and Scientific	PSLV-C32	successful
IRNSS-1G	28-04-2016	Mapping and Scientific	PSLV-C33	successful
CARTOSAT-2 & others	22-06-2016	Mapping and Scientific	PSLV-C34	successful
INSAT-3DR	08-09-2016	Meteorology	GSLV-F05	successful
SCATSAT-1 & others	26-09-2016	Multipurpose	PSLV-C35	successful
CARTOSAT-2 & 103 others	15-02-2017	Multipurpose	PSLV-C37	successful
GSAT-19	05-06-2017	Communication	GSLV-Mark-3D1	successful
CARTOSAT-2 & others	12-01-2018	Multipurpose	PSLV-C40	successful
IRNSS-1I	12-04-2018	Mapping and Scientific	PSLV-C41	successful
NovaSAR & S1-4	16-09-2018	Mapping	PSLV-C42	successful
Microsat-R	24-01-2019	Mapping	PSLV-C44	successful
Chandrayaan-2	22-07-2019	Mapping and Scientific	GSLV-MK-III	successful

❑❑

Indian History

Famous Sites of Indus Valley Civilization

Name of Site	Year of Excavation	River/ Sea coast	Discoverer
Harappa (Montgomery–Pakistan)	1921	Ravi River	Dayaram Sahney
Mohanjodaro (Larkana–Pakistan)	1922	Indus River	Rakhal Das Banerjee
Chanhudaro (Sindh–Pakistan)	1931	Indus River	N.G. Mazumdar
Alamgir pur (Meerut – U.P.)	1952-55	Hindan River	Yagyadatta Sharma
Ropar (Punjab)	1953	Sutlej River	Yagyadatta Sharma
Rangpur (Kathiabar–Gujarat)	1953	Bhabar River	Madho Swaroop Vatsa, Rang Nath Rao
Kotdigi (Sindh–Pakistan)	1953	Indus River	Fazal Ahmed Khan
Lothal (Ahmedabad-Gujarat)	1954	Bhogwa River	Rang Nath Rao
Kalibanga (Ganganagar–Rajasthan)	1961	Ghaggar	Brajwasi Lal
Surkotara (Kutch–Gujarat)	1967	Ghaggar River	Ravindra Singh Vishta
Banawali (Hissar Haryana)	1973	Ghaggar River	Ravindra Singh Vishta
Balakote	1979	Arabian Sea	George F. Dales
Dhaulavira (Gujarat)	1963-68	—	J.P. Joshi
	1990-91	—	Dr. R.S. Vishta

Wellknown Quotations

"Swarajya is My Birthright"	— Bal Gangadhar Tilak
"Give me blood, I shall give you freedom"	— Netajee Subhash Chandra Bose
"Inqalab Zindabad"	— Bhagat Singh
Saare Jahan Se Achcha, Hindustan Hamara"	— Dr. Mohammed Iqbal
"Dilli Chalo"	— Subhash Chandra Bose
"Sarfaroshi ki tamanna, Ab Hamare Dil Mein Hai."	— Ram Prasad Bismil
"I am socialist by nature".	— Jawahar Lal Nehru
"Go to Vedas"	— Swami Dayanand
"Aaram Haram Hai"	— Jawahar Lal Nehru
"Jai Jawan, Jai Kisan"	— Lal Bahadur Shastri
"Jai Jawan, Jai Kisan, Jai Vigyan"	— Atal Bihari Vajpayee
"Speak less, work more"	— Sanjay Gandhi

"Vijayee Vishwa Tiranga Pyara"	— Shyam Lal Gupta
"Quit India"	— Mahatma Gandhi
"Hindi, Hindu, Hindustan"	— Bhartendu Harishchandra
"Purna Swarajya"	— Jawahar Lal Nehru
"Every lathi blow inflicted on my body will prove a nail in British coffin"	— Lala Lajpat Rai
"Jai Hind"	— Subhash Chandra Bose
"Do or die"	— Mahatma Gandhi
"Who lives if India dies"	— Jawahar Lal Nehru
"Vande Mataram"	— Bankim Chandra Chatterjee
"Jana Gana Mana Adhinayaka Jai Hai"	—Rabindranath Tagore
"Hate sin, not the sinner."	— Mahatma Gandhi
"Service of the people is the service of God"	— Swami Vivekananda
"Truth and non-violence are my God."	— Mahatma Gandhi

Battles and Wars In India

War	*Year*	*Result*
Battle of Kalinga	(261 B.C.)	Ashoka defeated the king of Kalinga
Second battle of Tarain	(1192 A.D.)	Muhammad Gori defeated Prithviraj Chauhan
First battle of Panipat	(1526 A.D.)	Babar defeated Ibrahim Lodi
Battle of Khanwa	(1527 A.D.)	Babar defeated Rana Sanga
Battle of Chausa	(1539 A.D.)	Shershah Suri defeated Humayun and became ruler of Delhi
Second Battle of Panipat	(1556 A.D.)	Akbar defeated Hemu
Battle of Talikota	(1565 A.D.)	Allied forces of Bijapur, Bidar, Golkunda and Ahamadnagar defeated the King of Vijay Nagar
Battle of Haldighati	(1576 A.D.)	Rana Pratap was defeated by Akbar
Battle of Palasey	(1757 A.D.)	British forces defeated Nawab of Bengal Sirajudoulla
Battle of Wandiwash	(1760 A.D.)	British forces defeated the French
Third battle of Panipat	(1761 A.D.)	Maratha were defeated by Ahmad Shah Abadali
Battle of Buxar	(1764 A.D.)	British forces defeated the combined forces of Mir Quasim, Shah Alam Mughal empire and Awadh's Nawab
Third Anglo-Maratha War	(1792 A.D.)	Maratha were conclusively defeated
Fourth Anglo-Mysore War	(1799 A.D.)	Tipu Sultan died fighting the British forces
Second Anglo-Sikh War	(1848 A.D.)	British forces annexed Punjab from Sikh rulers
Indo-China War	(1962 A.D.)	China attacked India unilaterally and annexed some area
Indo-Pak War	(1965 A.D.)	Pakistan attacked India but had to suffer severe setbacks
Indo-Pak War	(1971 A.D.)	Pak declare war against India.

❏❏

Important Dates of Indian History

Important Dates of Indian History

B.C.

2500-1500 :	Indus Valley Civilization
1200-600 :	Vedic Era
563 :	Birth of Gautam Buddha; Nirvana 483 B.C.
540 :	Birth of Mahavir; Nirvana 468 B.C.
327-326 :	Alexander's invasion of India
321 :	Rise of Maurya Dynasty
273-232 :	Ashoka's Reign
58 :	Beginning of Vikrama Era

A.D.

78-120 :	Saka Era
320-540 :	Gupta Dynasty — the golden age of Hindu India
399-414 :	Visit of Fahien (Chinese Traveller)
606-647 :	Harsh Vardhana's reign; visit of Hiuen-Tsang—Chinese traveller
750 :	Pal Dynasty founded by Gopal
753 :	Rise of Rashtrakuta empire
846 :	Vijayalaya founded Chola Dynasty
1001 :	First invasion of India by Mahmud of Ghazni
1192 :	Mohammad Ghori defeated Prithviraj Chauhan at Tarain.
1206 :	Qutab-ud-din establishes slave Dynasty
1211 :	Accession of Iltutmish
1221 :	Chengiz Khan invades India
1265 :	Accession of Balban
1290 :	Khilji dynasty takes over in Delhi
1320 :	Ghiyas-ud-din Tughlaq establishes Tughlaq dynasty
1336 :	Rise of Vijayanagar empire
1398 :	Timur Lang invades India
1469 :	Birth of Guru Nanak; founder of Sikhism
1498 :	Discovery of sea-route to India by Vasco-da-Gama
1526 :	First Battle of Panipat; Babar founded the Moghul Empire
1530 :	Accession of Humayun
1540-55 :	Sur Empire
1556 :	Akbar ascends the throne

1565 : Battle of Talikota and destruction of Vijaya Nagar

1576 : Battle of Haldighati and defeat of Rana Pratap

1600 : East India Company established (Dec. 31)

1605 : Accession of Jahangir

1628 : Accession of Shahjahan

1658-1707 : Reign of Aurangzeb; Beginning of the end of the Moghul Empire

1739 : Nadir Shah invades India

1757 : Battle of Plassey, establishment of British Political rule in India

1761 : Third Battle of Panipat

1764 : Battle of Buxar (Bihar)

1835 : Macaulay recommended English to be the medium of instruction

1853 : First Railway Line opened in India

1857 : Indian Mutiny for Independence; Kolkata, Bombay and Madras Universities founded

1858 : British crown takes over the Administration of India.

1869 : Birth of Mahatma Gandhi

1885 : Indian National Congress founded

1889 : Pt. Jawaharlal Nehru born (Nov. 14)

1905 : Partition of Bengal

1911 : Transfer of capital of India from Calcutta to Delhi.

1919 : Jalianwala Bagh Tragedy (13th April)

1920 : Non-cooperation Movement started by Mahatma Gandhi

1928 : Simon Commission boycotted

1929 : Resolution for Purna Swaraj passed at the Lahore Congress under the Presidentship of Shri Jawaharlal Nehru (Dec.31)

1930 : Dandi March, First Round Table Conference

1931 : Irwin-Gandhi pact, 2nd Round Table Conference

1932 : Third Round Table Conference in London

1937 : Provincial Autonomy; Congress accepted Ministries in provinces

1942 : Arrival of Cripps in India; 'Quit India' resolution passed by Congress

1943-44 : Netaji Subhash Chandra   Bose forms Azad Hind Fauz

1947 : Division of India — India and Pakistan formed into separate Independent Dominions

1948 : Mahatma Gandhi assassinated (Jan.30)

1950 : Indian Constitution signed and adopted; India becomes a Sovereign Democratic Republic; Death of Sardar Patel

1951 : First Five Year Plan started

1952 : First General Elections in the country

1956 : States' Reorganisation Act, India divided into 14 States and 6 Union Territories

1961 : The Portuguese possessions in Goa, Daman and Diu liberated (December 18)

1962 : China's massive invasion of India (October 20); Emergency declared by the President (October 26)

1964 : Death of Prime Minister Jawaharlal Nehru (May 27)

1965 : Pakistan attacked the Indian territory at Kutch (April 24)

1966 : Taskent Agreement signed (Jan.10); Mr. Lal Bahadur Shastri died at Taskent (Jan 11); Mrs. Indira Gandhi became the Prime Minister of India (Jan 24); Indian currency devalued (June 6); New States of Punjab and Haryana came into being (Nov.1)

1969 : 14 big banks nationalised; Congress divided

1971 : General Insurance nationalised; Millions of Bangladesh refugees pour into India; Indo-Pak War; Emergency declared (December 3); Dhaka liberated by Indian Forces

1972 : India's N-East region re-organised — Meghalaya, Manipur and Tripura became full-fledged States; Mizoram and Arunachal Pradesh — the two new Union Territories came into being; Shimla Agreement

1973 : 24th Amendment to the Constitution empowering Parliament to amend any part of the Constitution including the Fundamental Rights held valid by the Supreme Court

1974 : India explodes nuclear device (May 18)

1975 : Sikkim became full-fledged State of India; First Indian satellite 'Aryabhatta' launched (April 19); Emergency declared due to internal disturbances (June 26); SITE launched (August 1)

1977 : Janata Party founded; 6th General Elections—Congress routed, first ever non-Congress government installed at the Centre

1978 : High denomination currency demonetized; Mrs Gandhi forms Congress (I)

1979 : Second satellite Bhaskara launched; Mr. Morarji Desai resigns as Prime Minister (July 15); Jaya Prakash Narain dead (October 8)

1980 : Massive win of Congress-I in Mid-term polls; Mrs. Gandhi again became the Prime Minister; Six more commercial banks nationalised

1982 : Ninth Asiad held in New Delhi

1984 : Sqn Ldr. Rakesh Sharma became first Indian to go into space through joint Indo-Soviet Space Mission (April 3-11); Metro Rail commences operation in Kolkata (Oct. 24); Assassination of Mrs. Indira Gandhi (Oct. 31)

1988 : Bill to reduce voting age to 18 passed by Parliament (Dec. 15)

1989 : India successfully launched 'Agni' (May 22); Testing of surface-to-surface missile 'Prithvi' successful (Sep 27); V P Singh sworn in as Prime Minister (Dec 2)

1990 : V P Singh's government voted out of power (Nov 7); Chandra Shekhar sworn in as PM (Nov. 10).

1991 : PM Rajiv Gandhi assassinated (May 21); P V Narasimha Rao sworn in as India's 9th PM (June 21).

1992 : Narasimha Rao elected Congress President (Feb 27); SD Sharma elected 9th President of India (July 16); Structure of Babri Masjid in Ayodhya demolished (Dec 6).

1993 : Autonomy for Bodo Areas (Feb 19); OBC job quota of 27% effective (Sep 8).

1994 : Panchayati Raj Act came into force (April 23); New telecom policy, allowing privatisation for basic telephone services announced (May 13).

1995 : Ban on sale of human organs (Feb. 4); INSAT-2C launched into orbit (Dec 7); IRS-1C put into orbit (Dec 28).

1996 : Enron Project revived (Jan 8); Atal Behari Bajpayee became PM (May 16); Popular Government installed in Jammu & Kashmir (Oct 9).

1997 : Rocket 'Pinaka' testfired successfully (Jan. 21); I.K. Gujral took over as India's 13th P.M. (April 21); INSAT-2D launched successfully (June 4); Shri K.R. Narayanan was sworn-in as President of India (July 25); INSAT-2D abandoned (Oct 5).

1998 : India conducts Nuclear Tests (May 11 and 13); Successful test flight of pilotless training aircraft (Sept. 3); formation of six member National Security Council (Nov 19).

1999 : PM Vajpayee's bus trip to Lahore (Feb 20); Indian armed forces start 'Operation Vijay' against Pakistani armed intruders crossing LOC in Kargil sector (May 25); Cyclone devastates Odisha and West Bengal (Oct 31).

2000 : INSAT-3B launched from Kourou (Mar 22); Jharkhand State bill passed by Rajya Sabha (Aug 10); Vishwanathan Anand become FIDE World Chess Champion (Dec 22).

2001 : Nishant India's unmanned aerial vehicle test flown (Jan. 31); GSLV-D1 launched (April 18); Terrorist attack on Parliament. All five militants killed (Dec. 13)

2002 : Mob attacked train in Gujarat, 58 died (February 27); Dr. A.P.J. Abdul Kalam sworn in as 12th President (July 25); Metro train service started in New Delhi (Dec. 24)

General Knowledge

2003 : Supersonic anti-ship cruise missile Brahmos test-fired successfully (Feb. 12); GSLV-D2 launched (May 8); India launches INSAT-3E from Kourou in French Guiana (Sep. 28).

2004 : Russian aircraft carrier 'Admiral Gorshkov' deal (Jan. 20); Maj RS Rathore got India its first individual silver in Athens Olympics (Aug. 17); South Coastal India hit by earthquake Tsunami (Dec. 26).

2005 : 20 States introduced VAT regime (April 1); Rural job Bill passed in LS (August 23); India, France inked $ 3.5 bn Scorpene deal (Oct. 6).

2006 : State Assam Changed its name to Asom (Feb. 27); India, US inked nuclear deal (March 2); India successfully carried out the first test of a cryogenic rocket engine (Oct. 28).

2007 : The Taj Mahel has been voted as one of the New Seven Wonders of the World (July 7); India clinched the inaugural ICC World Twenty-20 Championship (Sept. 24).

2008 : Abhinav Bindra won the Olympic Gold medal in Beijing for 10-metre air rifle event (Aug. 11); Moon Mission Chandrayan I lifted off successfully into its initial orbit (Oct. 22).

2009 : Brahmos cruise missile successfully test-fired (March 4); Manmohan Singh took oath as PM for second term (May 22); Dolphin declared national aquatic animal (Oct. 5).

2010 : Women Bill passed in Rajya Sabha (March 9); Rupee symbol '₹' cleared by Cabinet (July 15); XIX Commonwealth Games held in New Delhi (Oct. 3-14).

2011 : India joined the UN Security Council as non-permanent member (Jan. 2); Results of Census 2011 released: Puts India's population at 1.21 billion (March 31); India won World Cup Cricket 2011 (April 2); Sebastion Vettel won first Indian Grand Prix (Oct. 30).

2012 : India became 6th nation to have a nuclear submarine (Jan. 23); Supreme Court Scraps UPA's illigal 2G spectrum sale (Feb. 2); Pranab Mukherjee Sworn in as new President (July 25); China ready to resolve border issue with India (Dec. 1).

2013 : Afzal Guru hanged in Tihar Jail (Feb. 9); Manipur, Meghalaya & Tripura get High Courts (March 23); Direct benefit transfer for LPG Scheme launched in 18 districts of India (June 3); Centre notifies food security law (Sept. 15).

2014 : Prez Signs Lokpal Bill (Jan. 1); Narendra Modi takes oath as India's 15th PM (May 26); Telangana became 29th state of India (June 2); Bharat Ratna for Atal Behari Vajpayee and Madan Mohan Malviya (December 24).

2015 : NITI Aayog replaced Planning Commission with PM its Head (January 1); India, Srilanka set to intensify ties (September 15); India signs nuke MoU with Japan (Dec. 12).

2016 : New Juvenile Justice Act comes in force (Jan. 15); PM inaugurates 'Make in India' centre in Mumbai (Feb. 13); India conducts surgical strike along LOC in POK (Sept. 29). Modi's surgical hit on black money, ₹ 500, ₹ 1000 notes withdrawn (Nov. 8); Tamil Nadu CM J. Jayalalithaa passes away (Dec. 5).

2017 : Pravasi Bharatiya Divas held in Bengaluru (Jan. 7-9); Ram Nath Kovind Sworn in as 14th President (July 25); M. Venkaiah Naidu Sworn in as 13th Vice President of India (August 11); India won Asia Cup Hockey tournament (Oct. 22); Manushi Chhillar won the Miss World 2017 title (Nov. 18).

2018 : ISRO successfully launches navigation satellite IRNSS-1I (April 12); HD Kumaraswamy takes oath as Karnataka CM (May 23); J&K under Governor rule (June 20); India now 6th biggest economy, pips France (July 11); Former PM Atal Behari Vajpayee passes away (Aug. 16); PM launches India Post Payments Bank (IPPB) (Sept. 1); Ranjan Gogoi takes Oath as 46th CJI (Oct. 3).

2019 : PM inaugurates 106th Indian Science Congress in Jalandhar (Jan. 3); 10% EWS quota in jobs, education comes into effect (Jan 14); 15th Pravasi Bharatiya Divas Convention 2019 inaugurated in Varanasi (Jan. 22); India bombs Jaish Camp in Pakistan's Balakot (Feb., 26); Lok Sabha polls-2019 programme declared (March 10); Narendra Modi took oath as the Prime Minister for a second term (May 30); FM Nirmala Sitharaman presents her maiden Budget in Parliament (July 5); Moon Mission Chandrayan-2 lifted of successfully into its Orbit (July 22); Art. 370 scrapped, J&K loses its special status (Aug. 5); LS passes historic Bill on 2 new UTs in J&K (Aug. 6).

❑❑

World History

Important Historical Dates of the World

B.C.

776	: First Olympiad in Greece
323	: Alexander dies at Babylone
221	: Great Wall of China completed
4	: Birth of Jesus

A.D.

30	: Crucifixion of Jesus Christ
570	: Birth of Prophet Mohammed at Mecca
622	: Hizari era started, Hazrat Mohammad went from Macca to Madina
1453	: Renaissance in Europe
1492	: Columbus discovered America
1498	: Sea-route to India discovered (Vasco Da Gama)
1688	: Glorious Revolution in England, and the Parliamentary rule began
1776	: Declaration of American Independence (4th July)
1789	: French revolution
1804-25	: Industrial Revolution in England
1815	: Battle of Waterloo --- Napolean was defeated and sent to St. Helena where he died in captivity
1865	: Abraham Lincoln assassinated
1896	: Modern Olympic Games started in Athens
1904	: Russia-Japan war
1914-18	: World War I (Aug., 1914- Nov. 11, 1918)
1917	: Revolution in Russia, the Czar assassinated
1920	: The League of Nations founded
1933	: Hitler became the Chancellor of Germany
1939-45	: World War II
1945	: First Atom Bomb dropped on Hiroshima (Aug.6) and Nagasaki (Aug.9); UNO established (Oct.24)
1948	: Independence of Burma (4th January), Sri Lanka (6th February); Jews declared State of Israel in Palestine
1953	: Mt. Everest conquered by Hillary and Tenzing (May 29)
1957	: Artificial earth satellites (Sputniks I and II) launched by Russia
1963	: American president John F. Kennedy assassinated

1969 : American astronauts land on moon (July 21)

1973 : Watergate Scandal in U.S.A.; U.S.A. launched Skylab - the first Space Laboratory

1975 : Communists capture Cam-bodia and South Vietnam; Everest scaled by first woman Mrs. Juniko Tabei; a Japanese housewife; Coup in Bangladesh - Sheikh Mujib killed; Apollo-Soyuz joint flight

1976 : Unification of Vietnams; Death of Mr. Mao-tse Tung

1977 : America makes neutron bomb; Army seizes power in Pakistan

1978 : World's first test-tube baby born in England

1980 : Iran-Iraq war

1982 : Falkland war; Egypt regains Sinai peninsula

1984 : Hong Kong accord signed (UK-China)

1985 : SAARC comes into being in Dhaka

1986 : Fire in Russia's Chernobyl nuclear power plant.

1988 : Gorbachev elected USSR President; Bush elected US President.

1989 : Non-Communist government installed in Romania (Dec 25).

1990 : Nelson Mandela released after 27 years in prison (Feb 11); Namibia achieved independence (March 21); Two German states unite (Oct 3).

1991 : Gulf War started (Jan 17-Feb 27); Bangladesh reverted to the parliamentary form of government after 16 years (September); USSR dissolved (Dec. 21)

1992 : Boutrous Ghali elected new UN Secretary-General (Jan 1); Earth Summit at Rio de Janerio (June 12); Bill Clinton elected 42nd US President (Nov. 4).

1993 : Treaty to ban chemical weapons signed in Paris (Jan. 15).

1994 : GATT signed by 125 countries in Marrakesh (Morocco) on April 15; First non-white government in South Africa under Presidentship of Nelson Mandela (May 10).

1995 : WTO comes into existence (Jan. 1); First World Summit on social development in Copenhagen (March 6-12).

1996 : New Constitution in S. Africa (May 8); Atlanta Olympic (July 20-Aug 4); Kofi Annan of Ghana is the new UN Secretary General (Dec. 17).

1997 : Ninth SAARC Summit (May 12-14); NASA spacecraft Path-finder landed on Mars (July 4); Diana, Princess of Wales, killed in a car crash in Paris (Aug. 31).

1998 : Pakistan conducts Nuclear Tests (May 28); India, Russia sign nuclear agreement (June 21); The birth of Euro Currency (Dec 31).

1999 : NATO forces launch attack on Yugoslavia (Apr-May); Colonel Eileen Collins became the first women in the space history to command a space mission (July 23).

2000 : XXVIII Olympic Game starts in Sydney (Sept 15); European Union Army comes into being (Nov 20); George Bush elected President of USA (Dec. 16).

2001 : Nasa launched its 2001 Mars Odyssey probe form Kennedy Space Centre in Florida (April 7); World Trade Center and the Pentagon Headquarters in USA attacked by terrorists (Sep. 11).

2002 : The 11th SAARC summit held in Kathmandu (Nepal) (January 5-6); Xanana Gusnao become the first President of the World's 192nd independent state East Timor (May 20).

2003 : Space Shuttle Columbia of USA exploded, all the seven member including Kalpana Chawla of Indian origin died (Feb. 1); US attack on Iraq (March 19); Iran quake tolls mount to nearly 50,000. India to fly relief to Iran (Dec. 29).

2004 : Mars Exploration Rover Spirit rolled onto the Martian soil successfully (Jan. 15); Opportunity Probe Landed on Mars (Jan. 25); Earthquake Tsunami Killed thousands across nine nations (Dec. 26).

2005 : Bhutan unveiled its first constitution (March 26); Iraq's first elected government sworn in (May 3); Arab world's first Parliament met in Cairo (Dec. 27).

2006 : SAFTA became operational (Jan. 1); Nepal parliament stripped powers of king and turned secular (May 18); Ban Ki-moon elected UN Secretary General (Oct. 13); Saddam Hussain is executed (Dec. 30).

2007 : Japan launched first defence ministry since World War-II (Jan. 9); Australia won World Cup Cricket 2007 (continuous third time) (April 28); Time magazine named Russian President Vladimir Putin as "Person of the Year" for 2007 (Dec. 19).

2008 : Maoist leader Pushpa Kamal Dahal (Prachanda) becomes the first PM of Republican Nepal (August 15); 29th Olympic Games (8-24 August) ended in Beijing (August 24); Japan launched world's first solar cargo ship (Dec. 20).

2009 : Barack Obama sworn in as the 44th President of USA (Jan. 20); 15th NAM Summit held in Sharm-El-Shiekh (Egypt) (July 16); Russia launched new oil route to Asia (Dec. 28).

2010 : Dubai opened world's tallest skyscraper-Burj Khalifa (Jan. 4); 7.0 magnitude quake hit Haiti, more than Lakh died (Jan. 14); US, Russia signed nuclear arms pact (April 8); Russian Parliament approved new START (Dec. 24).

2011 : Dilma Rousseff sworn in as Brazil's first woman prez (Jan. 1); China tested first stealth jet (Jan. 11); US forces killed Osama-bin-Laden in Pakistan (May 1); 17th SAARC Summit held in Addu, Maldives (Nov. 10-11).

2012 : Myanmar pardons as number of prominent political prisoners (Jan. 13); 30th Olympic games (27th July to 12 August) ended in London (August 12); West Indies won Twenty-20 World Cup 2012 (Oct. 7); US president Barack Obama wins another term (Nov. 7); Spain gives peek at shipwreck treasure (Dec. 1).

2013 : UN Clinches global deal on cutting mercury emissions (Jan. 19); XI Jinping takes over as China's president (March 14); Hassan Rowhani sworn in as President of Iran (Aug. 4); North Korea restarts nuke reactor (Sept. 12); Nelson Mandela died (Dec. 5).

2014 : Sheikh Hasina is sworn in as Bangladesh PM for 3rd term (Jan. 12); Obama opens 9/11 museum (May 15); 18th SAARC Summit held in Kathmandu (November 26-27); UN declares June 21 as Yoga Day (Dec. 11).

2015 : Pope gives Lanka its 1st Saint (January 14); Australia lift ICC World Cup for a record 5th time (March 29); A massive earthquake hit Nepal, more than 5000 dead (April 25); Britain and Iran reopen embassies (August 23).

2016 : China's 2-child policy takes effect (Jan. 1); Eastern Russia rattled with 7.0 intensity earthquake (Jan. 30); On Earth Day, 171 countries sign climate deal (April 22); Iran, 6 nations release N-deal papers to public (Dec. 24).

2017 : Thailand King orders Constitution amendment (Jan. 10); Donald Trump sworn in as the 45th President of USA (Jan. 20); Pak Assembly passes Hindu marriage Bill (March 9); Federal Judge block Trump's new travel ban (March 16); Jacinda Ardern takes over as new New Zealand PM (Oct. 26); South Africa's Demi-Leigh Nel-Peters Crowned Miss Universe 2017 (Nov. 26).

2018 : US blocks $ 255 m. military aid to Pakistan (Jan. 2); French Parliament bans MPs from wearing any religious symbols (Jan. 25); End of Castros' 60-year rule in Cuba as Diaz-Canel takes over as new president (April 19); Vladimir Putin sworn in for fourth term as Russia President (May 7); Imram Khan takes Oath as Pakistan's 22nd PM (Aug. 18); Arif Alvi takes Oath as 13th Pakistan President (Sept. 9); North, South Korea agree to reconnect rail, road links (Oct. 15).

2019 : Brazil enters new era with far-right Prez Jair Bolsonaro (Jan. 1); Sheikh Hasina sworn in as Bangladesh PM for fourth term (Jan. 7); Malaysia scraps $ 6 billion China rail project (Jan. 27); EU adds UAE to tax haven blacklist (March 12); 49 killed in racial terror attack on 2 mosques in New Zealand (March 15); Scott Marrison sworn in as Australian PM (May 29); England won World Cup Cricket (July 14); US, Russia withdraw from cold war-era arms treaty (Aug. 2).

❑❑

General Knowledge

World Geography

Earth: The earth constitutes land, water and air. Land is made up of rocks and soil. It is distributed in continents and islands. The water found in oceans, seas, lakes, etc. occupies about 2/3 of the earth's surface. The earth is surrounded by a cover of air, called atmosphere, which extends up to several hundred kilometres above its surface.

Shape: In ancient times people believed that the earth was flat in shape. Greek philosopher Pythagoras (6th century BC) was the first person to declare that the earth was round. After careful measurement, the scientists have found that the earth is slightly oblate (flattened at poles) and not exactly round.

Motions: The earth has two motions: *(i) Rotation:* Earth makes a complete round on its axis once each 24 hours (more exactly 23 hours, 56 minutes and 4.09 seconds). It causes days and night on the earth. *(ii) Revolution:* The earth makes a complete round of the Sun in one year. This revolution of earth produces alternate seasons.

Some Facts: **(1)** Equal Day and Night — March 21 and September 23. **(2)** Longest Day — June 21. **(3)** Shortest Day — December 22. **(4)** The sunlight takes eight minutes in travelling from the Sun to the Earth. **(5)** Average speed of the earth in orbit — 66,600 miles (107,220 km) per hour. **(6)** Earth's equatorial diameter is about 7926 miles (12,756 km). **(7)** Water (oceans, seas, lakes and rivers) occupies nearly 75 per cent of the surface of the earth. **(8)** Earth's average distance from the Moon — 2,38,857 miles (3,84,400 km). **(9)** Earth's average distance from the Sun — 93 million miles (149.4 million km).

Greenwich Time: It is the local time of the Greenwich observatory in London on 0° meridian. Greenwich time is international standard time.

International Date Line: Half way round the earth from the Greenwich is International Date Line on 180° longitude. It runs down mid-Pacific. It is one day earlier on the east of this line than it is on the west of the line. When it is Monday east of the line, it is Tuesday west of the line.

Zones: On the basis of temperature and distribution of solar heat on the surface of the earth, the earth has been divided into five zones: (1) Torrid Zone, (2) North Temperate Zone, (3) South Temperate Zone, (4) Arctic Zone, and (5) Antarctic Zone.

Continents: Large land masses forming large geographical divisions are called continents. There are seven continents: (1) Asia (21.3%), (2) Africa (20.4%), (3) Europe (15.2%), (4) North America (14.0%), (5) South America (13.8%), (6) Australia (5.8%), and (7) Antarctica (9.6%).

Highest Mountain Peaks: (1) Everest (Asia-8848 metres), (2) Aconcagua (South America-6960 metres), (3) Mckinley (North America-6194 metres), (4) Kilimanjaro (Africa-5895 metres), (5) Elbrus (Europe-5642 metres), (6) Vinson Massif (Antarctica-5140 metres), (7) Kosciusko (Australia-2228 metres).

Largest Oceans: (1) Pacific Ocean (The largest, covers almost 1/3 of the earth's total area, and the deepest about 6.8 miles at Mariana Trench in western Pacific); (2) Atlantic Ocean, and (3) Indian Ocean. Other seas and gulfs are — the Mediterranean Sea, South China Sea, Bering Sea, Caribbean Sea, East China Sea, Sea of Japan, North Sea, Baltic Sea, Hudson Bay and Gulf of Mexico.

Longest Rivers: (1) Nile (6650 km-Africa), (2) Amazon (6437 km-South America), (3) Mississippi-Missouri (6020 km-North America), (4) Yangtze Kiang (5494 km-Asia), (5) Ob Irtysh (5410 km-Europe), (6) Congo (4666 km-Africa).

Great Deserts: (1) Sahara (94 lakh sq km-North Africa), (2) Libyan (11.65 lakh sq km-North Africa), (3) Australian (16 lakh sq km-Australia), (4) Gobi (13 lakh sq km-Mongolia), (5) Great Victoria (6,47,000 sq km-Australia), (6) Syrian (5,20,000 sq km-Arabia), (7) Arabian (23,30,000 sq km Arabia).

Largest Islands: (1) Greenland (21,75,600 sq km) (2) New Guinea (7,77,000 sq km), (3) Borneo (7,25,545 sq km), (4) Malagasy (5,90,000 sq km), (5) Baffin Island (4,76,070 sq km).

Highest Waterfalls: (1) Angel (807 m-Venezuela), (2) Mongefossen (774 m-Norway), (3) Kukenaam (610 m-Venezuela), (4) Ribbon (491 m-USA), (5) King George VI (487 m-Guyana), (6) Upper Yosemite (435 m-USA).

MAJOR PRODUCERS OF CROPS, MINERALS AND INDUSTRIAL GOODS

Coal	—	China, USA, UK, Germany, Russia, Australia and India
Cocoa	—	Ghana, South Africa, West Indies
Coffee	—	Brazil, Columbia
Copper	—	Chile, USA, Peru, Indonesia
Cotton	—	China, USA, Russia, Egypt, India, Brazil, Argentina, Pakistan
Gold	—	South Africa, Australia, Canada, South America, India
Grapes	—	France, Italy, Portugal, California (USA).
Iron	—	Brazil, China, Australia, India
Jute	—	India, Bangladesh
Manganese	—	China, South Africa, Brazil
Petroleum	—	Saudi Arabia, USA, Venezuela, Russia
Rice	—	China, India, Japan, Myanmar (Burma)
Rubber	—	Thailand, Malaysia, Indonesia, Sri Lanka
Silk	—	Japan, China, India
Silver	—	Mexico, USA, Russia, Peru, India
Steel	—	USA, Germany, Russia, UK
Tea	—	India, China, Sri Lanka, Kenya
Wheat	—	China, India, Russia, USA, Canada
Wool	—	Australia, Argentina, New Zealand, South Africa
Tobacco	—	China, USA, India, Brazil, Russia.

The Highest, Biggest and Longest in the World

Airport	Largest	King Fahd International Airport, Dammon (Saudi Arabia)
Animal	Tallest	Giraffe (Average height 6.09 m)
	Largest & Heaviest	Blue Whale (190 tonnes)
	Longest recorded	Boot lace Worm (55 m)
	Fastest	Cheetah (Approximately 100 km/hr)

Bay	*With max. shore line*	Hudson Bay (Canada: 12268 km)
	With maximum area	Bay of Bengal (India: 217 million hc)
Bridge	*Highest*	Sidu River Bridge (China 1627 ft)
Building	*Tallest*	Burj Khalifa in Dubai (818 meter)
Canal	*Big ship (longest)*	Suez Canal (160 km) *Busiest* Kiel Canal (North Sea)
Canyon/Gorge	*Deepest*	Hells Canyon, Snake River (Idaho : 7900 ft)
	Largest	Grand Canyon (Colarado River; USA; 446 km)
Church	*Largest*	Basilica of St. Peter (Vatican City Rome—Area 23000 sq. m.)
City	*Largest in Area*	Jiuquan Gansu, China (Area 1,67,996 Sq km)
Continent	*biggest*	Asia (31,845,872 km^2)
	Smallest	Australia Mainland (Area 76,17,930 km^2)
Country,	*Largest in Population*	China (over 137 crore)
	Largest in Area	Russia (17,098,242 sq. km)
	With largest electorate	India (over 80 crores)
	Smallest independent	State of Vatican City (0.44 km^2)
	With most land frontiers	China (16)
Dam	*Largest (concrete)*	Grand Coulee Dam (1272 m on Columbia River (Washington State, USA)
	Highest	Jinping-I (305 m)
Delta	*Largest*	Sundarban's Ganga-Brahmaputra delta (1,05,000 sq. km)
Desert	*Largest*	Sahara (N. Africa; maximum length 5,150 km EW; maximum width 3,200 km NS)
Diamond	*Largest*	The Cullinan (3106 carats)
Dome	*Largest*	Singapore National Stadium (310 m.)
Epic	*Longest*	Mahabharata
Fish	*Largest fresh water*	Plabeuk (China, Laos and Thailand)
	Most abundant	Bristle mouth
	Most venomous	Stone Fish (Indo-Pacific Waters)
Film	*Most Oscars*	Ben Hur (11 Oscars—1959); Titanic (11 Oscars 1998) The Lord of Rings : The Return of the King (11 Oscars—2003).
Fountain	*Tallest*	King Fahd's Fountain (Jeddah, Saudi Arabia)
Fruit	*Most nutritive*	Avocado (Vitamins A, C, E and Proteins; Central and South America)
	Least nutritive	Cucumber
Goldmine	*Largest in area*	Grasberg Mines (Fapua, Indonesia)
Gulf	*Largest*	Gulf of Mexico (1,544,000 sq. km)
Hotel	*Tallest*	JW Marriott Marquis, Dubai (355 meter, 77 Floor
Hotel	*Largest (with most rooms)*	Hotel Rossiya (Moscow; Russia; 12 storey; 3,200 rooms)
Island	*Biggest*	Greenland (now known as Kalaatdlit Nunaat—2,175,600 sq km)

(R-1641) GK–4

Lake	*Largest*	Caspian Sea (Azerbaijan, Russia, Iran border: 37.18 lakh km^2)
	Deepest	Baikal (Siberia)
	Largest (fresh water)	Superior Lake (USA—Canada border: 82,350 km^2)
Library	*Biggest*	United States Library of Congress (Washington D.C. founded in 1800, contains 101 million items)
	Biggest non-statutory	New York Public Library
Mountain	*Highest peak*	Mt. Everest (8848 m; Nepal)
	Highest range	Himalayas, Asia (upto 4200 m)
	Greatest mountain range	Himalaya-Karakoram (96 out of 109 peaks over 7315 m are here)
Museum	*Largest*	American Museum of Natural History, New York
Ocean	*Largest and Deepest*	The Pacific (Area: 166,240,000 km^2; Depth: 10,924 m)
Peninsula	*Largest*	Arabia (3.25 million sq. km)
Park	*Largest*	National Park of North-Eastern, Greenland (972000 km^2)
Places	*Coldest (annual mean)*	Polus Nedostupnosti (Antarctica −58°C)
	Driest (annual mean)	Desierto de Atacame (near Calama; Chile; rainfall nil)
	Hottest (annual mean)	Dallol (Ethiopia; 34.4°C mean temperature)
	Rainiest (annual mean)	Mowsynram near Cherapunji (Meghalaya; India; 11,873 mm)
	Windiest	The Commonwealth Bay (Gales reach 320 km/ph)
Planet	*Biggest*	Jupiter (equatorial diameter 142984 km)
	Brightest, hottest and nearest to Earth	Venus
	Nearest to Sun	Mercury
	Most satellites	Jupiter (63)
Plateau	*Highest*	Tibetan Plateau (Central Asia: 4900 m)
Platform	*Longest (rail)*	Gorakhpur (UP)
Port	*Largest*	Port of New York and New Jersey (USA)
Port	*Busiest*	Rotterdam (Netherlands)
Railway Line	*Longest*	Trans-Siberian Railway (Moscow-Nakhodka: 9438 km)
Railway Station	*Largest*	Grand Central Terminal (New York City; 19 hc)
	Highest	Condor (Bolivia; 4786 m)
Religion	*Oldest*	Hinduism
Religion	*Largest*	Christianity
Rivers	*Longest*	(i) Nile (6650 km) (ii) Amazon (6437 km)
Road	*Longest*	Pan American Highway (Alaska---Brasila: 48,000 km)
Sea	*Largest*	South China Sea (2,974,600 sq. km)
	Largest (inland)	Mediterranean
Stadium	*Largest*	Strahov Stadium at Prague (Czechoslovakia (240,000 spectators)
Star	*Brightest*	Sirius A (also called Dog Star)
Swimming course	*Longest recognised*	English Channel

Telescope	*Largest (radio)*	Five Hundred meter Apertune Spherical Telescope (FAST), China.
	Largest (solar)	Kitt Peak National Observatory, (Arizona; USA)
	Largest refractor	At Yerkes observatory (Wisconsin; USA; 18.9 m)
Temple	*Largest*	Angkor Vat (Cambodia: 402 acres)
Tower	*Tallest*	Sky Tree, Tokyo, Japan
Train	*Fastest*	Japan's magnetically levitated (magler) train (Speed over 500 km/hr)
Tunnel	*Longest (railway)*	Gotthard Base Rail Tunnel (Switzerland; 57.1 km)
	Largest (road)	Laerdal, Norway (24.51 km)
Volcano	*Greatest concentration in*	Indonesia
	Highest (extinct)	Cerro Aconcagua (6960 m; Andes)
	Highest (dormant)	Volcan Llullaillaco (6723 m; Argentina-Chile)
	Highest (active)	Ojos del Salado (Chile-Argentina)
Wall	*Longest*	Great Wall of China (main length 3460 km; branches length 2860 km)
Waterfall	*Highest*	Salto-Angel (in Venezuela on a branch of river Carrao, 807 m.)
	Widest	Khone Falls (Laos; width 10.8 km)
	Largest	Guaira (Brazil-Paraguay; on the Alto Parana River)
Zoo	*Largest*	Etosha Reserve (Namibia; area 10 million hc approx.).

First in the World

First Chinese visitor to India	Fahien
First foreign invader of India	Alexander, the Great (Greek)
First person to climb Mt. Everest	Tenzing Norgay (India) and Edmund Hillary (New Zealand) (1953)
First atom bomb dropped at	Hiroshima (Japan)
First man in the space	Yuri Gagarin (former USSR)
First woman in the space	Valentina Tereshkova (former USSR)
First person to walk in the space	Alexei Leonov (former USSR)
First person to land on the moon	Neil Armstrong (USA)
First and the only woman to have climbed Mt. Everest twice	Santosh Yadav (Indian; May 12, 1992; May 10, 1993)
First person on Mt. Everest without oxygen	Phu Dorjee (Indian; May 9, 1984)
First person to climb Mt. Everest twice	Nawang Gombu
First person to climb Mt. Everest maximum times	Chhewang Nima Sherpa (19 times)
First President of the USA	George Washington
First woman Prime Minister	Sirimavo Bandaranaike (Sri Lanka)
First person to swim across English Channel	Mathew Webb
First woman to swim across English Channel	Gertrude Caroline Ederle
First woman to climb Mt. Everest	Junko Tabei (Japan)
First woman to climb Mt. Everest alone and without oxygen supplies	Alison Hargreaves (Briton: May 13, 1995)

First Aeroplane to fly around the world without refuelling	Voyager (Dec. 1986)
First test-tube Baby	Louise Brown (UK; 1978)
First all-talking Film	Jaz Singer (1927)
First Secretary-General of the UN	Trygve Lie (Norway: 1946-53)
First woman President of the UN General Assembly	Vijayalakshmi Pandit (India: 1953)
First woman to reach North Pole	Ann Bancroft (1986)
First person to reach North Pole	Robert Peary
First person to reach South Pole	Amundsen (1911)
First woman to command Spacecraft in space	Ellin Collins

Popular Names

Popular Name	*Real Name*
Badshah Khan	Abdul Ghaffar Khan
Bapu, Father of Nation	M.K. Gandhi
Bard of Avon	William Shakespeare
Chachaji *or* Panditji	Jawaharlal Nehru
Desert Fox	Gen. Rommel (Germany)
Desh Bandhu	C.R. Das
Father of English Poetry	Geoffrey Chaucer
Fuhrer	Adolf Hitler
Grand Old Man of India	Dadabhai Naoroji
Grand Old Man of Britain	W.E. Gladstone
Gurudev	Rabindra Nath Tagore
Guruji	M.S. Golwalkar
Grand Commoner	Pitt, the younger
Iron Man of India	Sardar Patel
Lady with the Lamp	Florence Nightingale
Lal, Bal, Pal	Lala Lajpat Rai, Bal Gangadhar Tilak, Bipin Chandra Pal
Li-Kwan	Pearl Buck
Little Corporal *or* Man of Destiny	Napoleon Bonaparte
Lokmanya	Bal Gangadhar Tilak
Lok Nayak	Jayaprakash Narain
Mahamana	Pt. Madan Mohan Malaviya
Maid of Orleans	Joan of Arc
Maiden Queen	Queen Elizabeth I
Man of Blood and Iron	Prince Bismark
Netaji	Subhash Chandra Bose
Nightingale of India	Sarojini Naidu
Priyadarshini	Indira Gandhi
Punjab Kesari	Lala Lajpat Rai
Wizard of the North	Walter Scott

Geographical Surnames

Geographical Surname	Real Name
Bengal's Sorrow	Damodar River
Blue Mountains	Nilgiri Hills
China's Sorrow	Hwang-Ho
City of Palaces	Kolkata
City of Skyscrapers *or* Empire City	New York
City of Dreaming Spires	Oxford
Cockpit of Europe	Belgium
Dark Continent	Africa
Emerald Isle	Ireland
Eternal City	Rome
Forbidden City	Lhasa (Tibet)
Gateway of India	Mumbai
Gate of Tears	Strait of Bab-el-mandab
Gift of the Nile	Egypt
Granite City	Aberdeen (Scotland)
Hermit Kingdom	Korea
Holy Land	Jerusalem (Palestine)
Island of Pearls	Bahrain (Persian Gulf)
Island of Cloves	Zanzibar
Key to the Mediterranean	Gibraltar
Land of Five Rivers	Punjab
Land of Golden Pagoda	Myanmar (Burma)
Land of Kangaroo	Australia
Land of Maple Leaf/Lillies	Canada
Land of Midnight Sun	Norway
Land of Morning Calm	Korea
Land of the Rising Sun	Japan
Land of Thousand Lakes	Finland
Land of Thunderbolt	Bhutan
Land of the White Elephants	Thailand
Manchester of the Orient	Osaka (Japan)
Pearl of the Antilles *or* Sugar Bowl of the World	Cuba
Pink City	Jaipur
Playground of Europe	Switzerland
Queen of the Adriatic	Venice (Italy)
Roof of the World	Pamirs
Sick Man of Europe	Turkey
Venice of the North	Stockholm (Sweden)
Windy City	Chicago
Whiteman's Grave	Guinea Coast of Africa
World's Loneliest Island	Tristan de Cunha

Countries'/Cities' Names—Old and New

Old Name	New Name	Old Name	New Name
Abyssinia	Ethiopia	Leningrad	St. Petersburg
Basutoland	Lesotho	Leopoldville	Kinshasa
Bechuanaland	Botswana	Mesopotamia	Iraq
British Honduras	Belize	North Rhodesia	Zambia
Burma	Myanmar	Nyasaland	Malawi
Ceylon	Sri Lanka	Peking	Beijing
Zaire	Congo	Persia	Iran
Constantinople	Istanbul	Rangoon	Yangon
Dahomey	Benin	Salisbury	Harare
Dutch East Indies	Indonesia	Siam	Thailand
East Pakistan	Bangladesh	South West Africa	Namibia
Formosa	Taiwan	Southern Rhodesia	Zimbabwe
Gold Coast	Ghana		

Religious Population of the World (Mid-2015)*

Religion	Population	%
Christians	2,447,988,000	32.9
Roman Catholics	1,242,461,000	16.7
Protestants	552,599,000	7.4
Independents	428,591,000	5.8
Orthodox	284,117,000	3.8
Muslims	1,752,045,000	23.6
Hindus	1,019,421,000	13.7
Buddhists	521,492,000	7.0
Chinese folk religionists	441,145,000	5.9
Ethnoreligionists	267,226,000	3.6
Neoreligionists	66,451,000	0.9
Sikhs	25,741,000	0.3
Jews	14,778,000	0.2
Spiritists	14,550,000	0.2
Taoists	8,691,000	0.1
Baha'is	8,010,000	0.1
Confucianists	8,498,000	0.1
Jains	6,016,000	0.1
Shintoists	2,816,000	0.0
Zoroastrians	196,000	0.0
Nonreligious	827,599,000	11.1
Agnostics	691,289,000	9.3
Atheists	136,310,000	1.8
Total Population	**8,260,261,000**	**100.0**

World Almanac 2018

Airlines and Airports

Important Airlines

- AI — Air India
- British Airways — Britain
- JAL — Japan Airlines
- KLM — Royal Dutch Airline
- PAN AM — Pan American Airways
- PIA — Pakistan International Airlines
- SIL — Singapore International Airlines
- Lufthansa — German Airlines
- AEROFLOT — Russian Airlines
- Cathay Pacific — Hongkong Airlines
- Garuda — Indonesian Airlines
- TWA — Trans World Airlines (Private US Company)
- QUANTAS — Australian Airlines
- SAS — Scandinavian Airlines

Important Airports

- Britain — Heathrow (London)
- Japan — Narita and Haneda (Tokyo)
- America — Kennedy Air Port (New York)
- France — Charles de Gaulle (Paris)
- India — Indira Gandhi International Airport (New Delhi)
- Russia — Sheremetyevo (Moscow)
- Sweden — Arlanda (Stockholm)

Important Residences

● **Buckingham Palace (London):** King/Queen of Britain ● **10, Downing Street (London):** Prime Minister, Britain ● **Elysee Palace (Paris):** President, France ● **Rashtrapati Bhawan (New Delhi):** President, India ● **White House (Washington):** President, USA ● **Vatican (Rome):** Pope

Important towns situated on the River Banks

Town	River	Town	River
Agra	Yamuna	Karachi	Indus
Ahmedabad	Sabarmati	Lahore	Ravi
Prayagraj	Confluence of the Ganga and the Yamuna	Leh	Indus
		London	Thames
Ayodhya	Saryu	Lucknow	Gomati
Baghdad	Tigris	Nasik	Godavari
Berlin	Spree	New York	Hudson
Cairo	Nile	Paris	Seine
Kolkata	Hooghly	Patna	Ganga
Cuttack	Mahanadi	Rome	Tiber
Delhi	Yamuna	Srinagar	Jhelum
Dibrugarh	Brahmaputra	Surat	Tapti
Dublin	Liffey	Sydney	Murray-Darling
Hardwar	Ganga	Varanasi	Ganga
Hyderabad	Musi	Vienna	Danube
Jabalpur	Narbada	Washington	Potamac
Kanpur	Ganga	Yangon	Irawadi

Books and Authors

FOREIGN

Book	Author	Book	Author
Aesop's Fables	Aesop	Moor's Last Sigh	Salman Rushdie
Adventure of Robinson Crusoe	Daniel Defoe	Mother	Maxim Gorky
		Mother India	Katherine Mayo
Adventures of Sherlok Holmes	Arthur Conan Doyle	Nana	Emile Zola
		Ninteen Eighty Four	George Orwell
Alice in Wonderland	Lewis Carrol	Odyssey	Homer
Apple Cart	G.B.Shaw	Origin of Species	Charles Darwin
Arabian Nights	Sir Richard Burton	Othello	William Shakespeare
As You Like It	William Shakespeare	Paradise Lost	John Milton
A Tale of Two Cities	Charles Dickens	Paradise Regained	John Milton
A Tale of Two Gardens	Octavio Paz	Path to Power	Margaret Thatcher
A Thousand Suns	Dominique Lapierre	Pickwick Papers	Charles Dickens
August Coup	Mikhail S. Gorbachev	Pride and Prejudice	Jane Austen
Ben Hur	Lewis Wallace	Razor's Edge	Somerset Maugham
Candida	G.B. Shaw	Republic	Plato
Das Kapital	Karl Marx	Romeo and Juliet	William Shakespeare
David Copperfield	Charles Dickens	Round the World in Eighty Days	Jules Verne
Divine Comedy	A. Dante		
Doctor's Dilemma	G.B. Shaw	Rubaiyat-i-Omar Khayyam	Edward Fitzgerald (Translator)
Famished Road	Ben Okri		
Freedom From Fear	Aung San Suu Kyi	Shape of Things to Come	H.G. Wells
Gulistan Bostan	Sheikh Saadi		
Gulliver's Travels	Jonathan Swift	The Satanic Verses	Salman Rushdie
Hamlet	William Shakespeare	The Social Contract	Rousseau
Iliad	Homer	The Tempest	William Shakespeare
Inferno	A. Dante	Time Machine	H.G. Wells
In Memoriam	Lord Tennyson	Tom Sawyer	Mark Twain
Ivanhoe	Walter Scott	Treasure Island	R.L. Stevenson
Julius Caesar	William Shakespeare	Twelfth Night	William Shakespeare
Lady Chatterley's Lover	D.H. Lawrence	Uncle Tom's Cabin	H.B.Stowe
		Unto This Last	John Ruskin
Lajja	Taslima Nasreen	Utopia	Thomas More
Les Miserable	Victor Hugo	Universe Around Us	James Jeans
Leviathan	Thomas Hobbes	Vicar of Wakefield	Oliver Goldsmith
Lolita	V. Nobokov	War and Peace	Leo Tolstoy
Lycidas	John Milton	Wealth of Nations	Adam Smith
Mein Kampf	Adolf Hitler	Wonder That was India	A.L. Basham
Merchant of Venice	William Shakespeare		
Midnight's Children	Salman Rushdie	Wuthering Heights	Emily Bronte

INDIAN

Book	Author	Book	Author
Abhigyan Shakuntalam	Kalidas	Anand Math	Bankim Chandra Chatterjee
Ain-i-Akbari	Abul Fazal	Arthashastra	Kautilya

Book	Author	Book	Author
A Suitable Boy	Vikram Seth	Mati Matal	Gopi Nath Mohanty
Bhagwat Gita	Ved Vyas	Meghdoot	Kalidas
Chidambara	Sumitranandan Pant	Meri Ekyavan Kavitain	Atal Behari Vajpayee
Devdas	Sarat Chandra Chatterjee	Meri Sansadiya Yatra	Atal Behari Vajpayee
Diwan-i-Ghalib	Mirza Ghalib	Mritunjaya	B.K. Bhattacharya
Discovery of India	Jawaharlal Nehru	Mudrarakshasa	Vishakhadatta
Essays on Gita	Aurobindo Ghosh	My Experiments with Truth	M.K. Gandhi
Eternal India	Indira Gandhi		
Faces of Everest	Major H.P.S. Ahluwalia	My Own Boswell	M. Hidayatullah
Ganadevata	Tarashankar Bandopadhyaya	My Presidential Years	R. Venkataraman
Geet Govind	Jaya Dev	Nisheeth	Uma Shankar Joshi
Geetanjali	R. N. Tagore	'No, Sir'	P.G. Mavlankar
Glimpses of World History	Jawaharlal Nehru	One Day Wonders	Sunil Gavaskar
		Panchtantra	Vishnu Sharma
Godaan	Prem Chand	Passage to England	Nirad C. Chaudhuri
Gul-e-Nagma	Firaq Gorakhpuri	Prison Diary	Jaya Prakash Narayan
Gunahon ka Devta	Dharmveer Bharti		
Harsh Charita	Bana Bhatta	Raghuvansha	Kalidas
Hindu View of Life	S. Radhakrishnan	Rajtarangini	Kalhana
Idols	Sunil Gavaskar	Ramayana	Balmiki
India Divided	Dr. Rajendra Prasad	Ramcharit Manas	Tulsidas
The Judgement	Kuldip Nayyar	Rukh Te Rishi	Harbhajan Singh
Juhi ki Kali	Surya Kant Tripathi 'Nirala'	Satyarth Prakash	Swami Dayanand
		Sur Sagar	Surdas
Justice of Peace ke Aansu	Janardan Prasad Singh	The Guide	R.K. Narayan
Chand ka Munh Terha Hai	Muktibodh	The Insider	P.V. Narasimharao
		The Post Office — Dak Ghar	Rabindra Nath Tagore
Kapalkundala	Bankim Chandra Chatterjee	The God of Small Things	Arundhati Roy
Kadambari	Bana Bhatta	Urvashi	Ram Dhari Singh 'Dinkar'
Kagaz Te Kanwas	Amrita Pritam		
Kamayani	Jai Shankar Prasad	Yama	Mahadevi Verma
Kitni Nawon	S. H. Vatsyayan	My Country : My Life (Autobiography)	L.K. Advani
Kumar Sambhav	Kalidas		
Mahabharata	Ved Vyas	The Test of My Life	Yuvraj Singh
Malgudi Days	R.K. Narayan	Twenty Years in a Decade	Shah Rukh Khan
Manvini Bhavai	Pannalal Patel		

IMPORTANT BOOKS WRITTEN IN JAIL

Book	Author	Book	Author
My Experiments with Truth	Mahatma Gandhi	Pilgrim's Progress	John Bunyan
Glimpses of World History	Jawaharlal Nehru	Bible (in German language)	Martin Luther
Discovery of India		Les Miserables	Victor Hugo
Gita Rahasya	Lokmanya Bal Gangadhar Tilak	Long Walk to Freedom	Nelson Mandela

First in India

First in India

Nobel Prize for Literature (1913)	Rabindra Nath Tagore
Nobel Prize for Physics (1929)	C.V. Raman
Nobel Prize for Peace (1979)	Mother Teresa
Nobel Prize for Economics (1998)	Amartya Sen
Special Oscar award winner (1992)	Satyajit Ray
Governor-General of free India (Last also)	C. Rajagopalachari
Woman Governor of the State	Smt. Sarojini Naidu
Indian Chief of the Army Staff*	General K.M. Cariappa
Woman Chief Minister of a State	Smt. Sucheta Kripalani
Woman President of United Nations General Assembly (1954)	Smt. Vijaylakshmi Pandit
President of International Court of Justice	Dr. Nagendra Singh
Woman to swim across the English Channel	Ms. Aarti Saha
Miss Universe	Miss Sushmita Sen
Miss World	Reita Faria
Indian to swim across the English Channel	Mihir Sen
Field Marshal	S.H.F.J. Manekshaw
Indian recipient of Victoria Cross	Khudadad Khan
Indian to conquer Mt. Everest	Sherpa Tenzing, May 29, 1953
Indian male cosmonaut (1984)	Rakesh Sharma
Indian female cosmonaut	Kalpana Chawla (19 Nov., 1997)
Woman to climb Mt. Everest	Miss Bachendri Pal, May 23, 1984
Woman to get Olympic Medal	Karnam Malleswari
Indian to address the UN General Assembly in Hindi	Atal Behari Vajpayee
Newspaper	Bengal Gazette, Jan 27, 1780
Postage Stamp issued	In 1852
Telegraph line laid	In 1851, Kolkata; Diamond Harbour
Railways run	April 16, 1853; Bombay-Thana
Electric Train run	1925: Bombay-Kurla
Atomic Power Station	Tarapore (Maharashtra)
Passenger-cum-cargo ship made in India	Harshavardhan
Satellite	Aryabhatta (1975)
Rocket	Rohini (1967)

Atomic Reactor	Apsara (1956)
Climb Everest without oxygen	Phu Dorjee (1987)
First film (movie)	Raja Harishchandra (1913)
First film (talkie)	Alam Ara (1931)
Metro Railway	Kolkata Metro Railway
Test-tube baby, scientifically documented	Born on August 6, 1986 at K.E.M. Hospital, Mumbai
TV Centre	At Delhi
Indian to get an Oscar	Bhanu Athaiya
Woman pilot in IAF	Ms Harita Kaur Deol
Cellular Phone	Kolkata, August 1, 1995
Women president of Indian National Congress	Smt. Annie Besant
President of Indian National Congress	W.C. Banerjee (1885)
Indian who passed in I.C.S. Examination	Satendra Nath Tagore
Woman chief justice of High Court	Lila Saith (Himachal Pradesh)
Woman Foreign Secretary	Chokila Iyyar

First Important Officials of India

The Governor-General of free India	Lord Mountbatten
President	Dr. Rajendra Prasad
President (Female)	Pratibha Patil
Vice-President	Dr. S. Radhakrishnan
Prime Minister	Jawahar Lal Nehru
Prime Minister (Female)	Indira Gandhi
Deputy Prime Minister	Sardar Vallabhbhai Patel
Chief Justice	Harilal J. Kania
First Female Judge in Supreme Court	Smt. Meera Sahib Fatima Bibi
Speaker, Lok Sabha	Ganesh Vasudeo Mawlankar
Woman Speaker of Lok Sabha	Meira Kumar
Chief Election Commissioner	Sukumar Sen
Commander-in-Chief	General Sir Roy Bucher
Chief of Army Staff	General Maharaj Rajendra Sinhji
Chief of Air Staff	Air Marshal Sir Thomas Elmhirst
Chief of Naval Staff	Vice Admiral Ramdas Katari
Female Minister	Raj Kumari Amrit Kaur (Health Minister)
Female Governor	Sarojini Naidu (U.P.)
Female Chief Minister	Sucheta Kripalani (U.P. 1963)
Finance Commissioner	K.C. Niyogi
Leader of Opposition in Lok Sabha (Recognised)	Y.V. Chavan (Congress)
Leader of Opposition in Rajya Sabha (Recognised)	Kamalapati Tripathi (Congress)

Highest, Biggest, Largest & Longest in India

Award for Gallantry, Highest	Param Vir Chakra
Award, highest civilian	Bharat Ratna
Bank with largest number of branches	State Bank of India (24,000 branches till April 2017)

River bridge, Longest	Bhupen Hazarika Setu (across Lohit River: Assam 9.15 km)
Cantilever Span Bridge, Largest	Howrah Bridge (Kolkata)
Cattle Fair, Largest	Sonepur Fair (Bihar)
City, Most Populous	Mumbai
Corridor, Longest	Ramanathaswamy Corridor, Tamil Nadu (1,220 mt.)
Desert, Largest	Thar (Rajasthan)
Dam, Longest	Hirakud Dam (Odisha)
Dam, Highest	Tehri Dam on Bhagirathi river in Uttarakhand (855 ft.)
Delta, Largest	Sunderban (12,872 Sq. km.)
Dome, Largest	Gol Gumbaz (Bijapur)
Gateway, Highest	Buland Darwaja at Fatehpur Sikri (54 m.)
Lake, Largest (fresh water)	Wular Lake (Kashmir)
Literacy, Highest	Kerala
Museum, Largest	Indian Museum (Kolkata)
Mosque, Biggest	Jama Masjid (Delhi)
Peak, Highest	K-2 (8,611 mt.)
Railway Platform, Longest	Gorakhpur, UP
River, Longest	The Ganga river (2,525 km.)
Rainfall, Highest (annual mean)	Mowsynram near Cherrapunji (1,080 mm) (Meghalaya)
Road, Longest	Grand Trunk Road
Rock-cut Temple, Largest	KailashTemples, Ellora (Maharashtra)
State, maximum forest cover	Mizoram (cover 88.63% area)
State, Largest (area)	Rajasthan (3,42,239 sq. km.)
State, Most Populous	Uttar Pradesh (19,95,81,477)
State with Maximum density of population	Bihar (1102 persons per sq. km.)
Tunnel, Longest (Road)	Chenani-Nashri Tunnel (J & K—9.28 km)
Tunnel, Longest (Railway)	Qazigund Town in Kashmir to Banihal in Jammu (11.2 kms).
Tower, Highest	Qutub Minar (Delhi, 72.5 mt.)
Waterfall, Highest	Gersoppa Waterfall, Mysuru (290 m.)
Zoo, Largest	Zoological Gardens, Kolkata
Man-made Lake, Largest	Govind Sagar (Bhakra)

Principal Manufacturing Industries in India

Cotton Textile Industry	: Maharashtra, Gujarat, Tamil Nadu, U.P., W.Bengal, M.P., Karnataka, Kerala, Delhi (Maximum number of mills in Maharashtra).
Jute Industry	: West Bengal, Bihar, Asom, Andhra and Odisha.
Sugar Industry	: U.P., Bihar, Maharashtra, Tamil Nadu.
Silk Industry	: Karnataka, Murshidabad (W.Bengal), Srinagar, Asom, Bihar.
Woollen Industry	: Amritsar, Ludhiana, Dhariwal, Kanpur, Panipat.
Paper Industry	: Titagarh, Mumbai, Saharanpur, Jagadhri, Dalmia Nagar, Punalur (Kerala).
Chemical Industry	: Mumbai, Kolkata, Delhi, Kanpur, Amritsar, Chennai, Bangaluru
Antibiotic Factory	: Pimpri near Pune (Maharashtra), Rishikesh (Uttarakhand).
Glass Industry	: Ferozabad & Bahjoi (U.P.), Mumbai, W.Bengal, Amritsar (Punjab).

Aluminium Industry	:	Renukoot (U.P.), Kerala, W.Bengal, Jharkhand, Maharashtra, M.P.
Ship-building Industry	:	Visakhapatnam, Mumbai, Kolkata, Kochi
Cement Industry	:	Porbander, Katni (M.P.), Lakheri (Rajasthan), Vijayawada, Dadri (Haryana), Churk (U.P.), Banjari (Bihar).
Locomotive Industry	:	Chittaranjan Locomotive Works (W.Bengal) and Diesel Locomotive Works Varanasi (U.P.), Diesel Components Works Patiala (Punjab).
Heavy Electrical	:	Bhopal (M.P.), Hardwar (Uttarakhand), Hyderabad (A.P.), Tiruverumbur (Tamil Nadu).
Hindustan Machine	:	Jalahalli (Bengaluru), Pinjore (Chandigarh), Kalamassery (Kerala), Kukatpalli (Hyderabad), Zainkot, Srinagar (J&K).
Hindustan Teleprinters	:	Bangaluru and Chennai.
Coach Factory	:	Integral Coach Factory, Perambur (TN), Railway Coach Factory in Kapurthala (Punjab).
Lignite Factory	:	Neyvelli (Tamil Nadu).
Telephone Industry	:	Bengaluru (Karnataka).
Petroleum Industry	:	The present refining capacity in the country as on 1st June 2013 was 213.066 Million Metric Tonnes Per Annum (MMTPA). Out of 22 refineries operating in the country, 17 are in public sector, 3 are in private sector and 2 are in JV (Joint venture) of Public Sector.
Iron and Steel Industry	:	(i) Rourkela Steel Plant: Odisha-German collaboration; (ii) Bhilai Steel Plant: Chattisgarh — Russian collaboration; (iii) Durgapur Steel Plant: W.Bengal — British collaboration; (iv) Bokaro Steel Plant: Jharkhand — Russian collaboration; (v) Indian Iron & Steel Co. — Burnpur & Kulti — Nationalised in July 1975; and (vi) Tata Iron and Steel Works: Jamshedpur — In the Private Sector.

Indian Banks

- **Reserve Bank of India:** It was established in 1935 and nationalised in 1949. It is the Central Bank of the country and issues all currency notes except one rupee note. It acts as a banker to the Government and exercises control over other commercial banks in the country. Headquarters of Reserve Bank of India is in Mumbai.
- **The State Bank of India:** Largest commercial bank, which merged five of its associate banks and Bharatiya Mahila Bank on April 1, 2017, Joined the league of top 50 banks globally in terms of assests. Now State Bank of India have more than 24,000 branches in India and world.
- **Nationalisation of Banks:** The Government of India on July 19, 1969, took over 14 biggest commercial banks incorporated in the country. On April 15, 1980, six more banks were nationalised. In March 1994, the Parliament passed the Banking Regulation (Amendment) Bill, 1994 which inter alia provided for establishment of private sector banks.

Insurance

- **Life Insurance Corporation of India:** Since September 1, 1956, when the L.I.C. of India was established, life insurance business in India is transacted by the Corporation and, in a restricted sphere by the Posts and Telegraphs Department of the Government of India and by some State Governments.
- **General Insurance Corporation of India:** It was established in November, 1972 and with effect from January, 1974 the erstwhile 107 Indian and Foreign insurers were grouped by this corporation into four operation companies, namely National Insurance, New India Assurance, Oriental Insurance and United India Insurance. ❑❑

Cultural Activities

AKADEMIES

There are three akademies for promotion of creative art.

1. **Lalit Kala Akademi, New Delhi:** Established in 1954, the Lalit Kala Akademi strives for the popularisation of Indian art within the country and in various countries of the world through exhibitions, publications, workshops and camps. Every three year it organises the Triennale India, an international exhi-bition. It publishes research papers on Indian arts. Besides organising seminars, it honours eminent artists. The Akademi has set up regional centres called Rashtriya Lalit Kala Kendras at Lucknow, Kolkata, Chennai and Bhubaneswar and a small office at Mumbai.

2. **Sangeet Natak Akademi, New Delhi:** The Sangeet Natak Akademi, set-up in 1953, aims at the promotion and development of dance, drama and music. It holds seminars and festivals, presents awards to the eminent artists and extends financial assistance to traditional teachers and scholarships to students. It also operates a scheme of exchange of troupes.

3. **Sahitya Akademi, New Delhi:** The Sahitya Akademi, established in 1954, has the main functions of development of Indian letters, setting up high literary standards, translation of literary works of one Indian language into other Indian languages, publication of books on history of literature and criticism, bibliographies and reference books. The Akademy has regional offices at Mumbai,Kolkata, Bengaluru and Chennai.

4. **National School of Drama:** It is one of the top theatre training institutes in the world and only one of its kind in India. It was set up in 1959 under Sangeet Natak Akademi but was later made autonomous organisation in 1975.

SCULPTURE

Archaeological Survey of India, set up in 1861, is responsible for preservation and maintenance of sculptures and historical monuments and manages a number of archaeological museums.

National Archives of India, established in 1891, it is the official custodian of all non-current records of permanent value of the Government of India and its predecessor bodies.

MUSEUMS

They are repositories of the cultural heritage and conserve and preserve historical technical and other materials against decay and transmit them to posterity as records of history.

MUSIC

Main Schools of Classical Music: There are two main schools of classical music, namely, the Hindustani and the Carnatic. The Hindustani school of classical music is in vogue in north-western India, eastern India and northern parts of the South India.

Musical Instruments: They are: Tabla, Mridangam, Pakhawaj, Chandai, Dholak, Veena, Sitar, Sarod, Gootuvadhyam, Sarangi, Flute, Nadaswaram, Shehnai, Shringi and Turahi.

DANCE

India has a very rich tradition of tribal, folk and classical dances.

CLASSICAL DANCE

Dance	State	Famous Artists
Bharat Natyam	Tamil Nadu	Yamini Krishnamurthy, Rukmini Devi Arundale, Swapna Sundari, Sonal Mansingh, Vaijanti Mala, Mrinalini Sarabhai, Chandralekha, Indrani, Ram Gopal, Bal Saraswati
Kathakali	Kerala	Gopinath, K.K. Nayar, Kunju-Kurup, T.K. Chandu
Kuchipudi	Andhra Pradesh	Sapna Sundari, Raja Reddy, Shobha Nayar, Radha Reddy, Vedantam Satyanarayan, Vimpanti Chinna Satyam.
Kathak	North India	Birju Maharaj, Gopi Krishna, Shambhu Maharaj, Sitara Devi, Vishnu Sharma, Durga Lal, Shobhana Narayan
Odissi	Odisha	Kelucharan Mahapatra, Indrani Rehman, Madhavi Mudgal, Pratima Bedi, Samyukta Panigrahi, Sonal Mansingh, Debudas
Manipuri	Manipur	Uday Shankar, Bipin Singh, Suryamukhi, Darohra Jhaveri

FAMOUS FOLK-DANCE

State	Folk Dance	State	Folk Dance
Andhra Pradesh/ Telangana	Dandari, Banjara	Madhya Pradesh	Lota Nritya, Jawara
Assam	Bihu, Keli Gopal, Sataria	Maharashtra	Tamasha, Dahi Handi, Gof, Deepak Dindi
Bihar	Chhau, Magahi, Durga dance	Manipur	Dhol Cholam
W. Bengal	Kirtan, Kalatri, Asweabadh, Brita, Kalidance	Meghalaya	Nongakarem
Chhattisgarh	Saila, Karama, Bhagoria	Nagaland	Bamboo dance
Gujarat	Garba, Rasalila, Tippani, Dandia,	Odisha	Chhau, Maya Shabari, Dalachai
Haryana	Damyal, Lahoor	Punjab	Gidda, Bhangra, Panihari
Himachal Pradesh	Dussehra dance, Hikat, Notio	Rajasthan	Thumar, Kathaputali, Tera Tali
Jammu & Kashmir	Dumhal	Tamil Nadu	Terukalathu, Kabalatam, Kargam, Pulivesham
Jharkhand	Jhau, Ghumakudia, Jadur, Sarhul, Soharai, Karama, Vaima, Loojhari, Jat-Jatin, Vidayat	Tripura	Hazagiri
		Uttar Pradesh	Rasalila, Nautanki, Thali, Dhurang, Jhumela, Huraka, Bol.
Karnataka	Yakshagan, Dolu Kunitha	Uttarakhand	Kajari, Karan
Kerala	Mohini Attam, Padayuni	Goa	Dhode Modini

Musical Instrument	Artists	Musical Instrument	Artists
Flute	Hari Prasad Chaurasia, Panna Lal Ghosh, T.R. Mahalingam, N. Ramani, Vijaya Raghava Rao	Sitar	Pandit Ravishankar, Vilayat Khan
		Santur	Shiv Kumar Sharma
		Rudraveena	Zia Mohiuddin Dagar
Tabla	Allah Rakha, Gudai Maharaj, Latif Khan, Zakir Hussain	Pakhawaj	Govind Rao, Anokhe Lal, Kanthi Maharaj
Violin	Lalgudi Jayaraman, L. Subramaniam,, M.S. Gopal Krishnan, S. Subrahmaniam, V.G. Jog, N. Rajan	Mridanga	Palghat R. Raghu, U.S. Burman
		Harmonium	Purushottam Walawakar, M. Dhaulpuri
Shehnai	Bismilla Khan, Imrat Khan	Guitar	Pt. Vishnu Mohan Bhatt, Brij Bhushan Kalra
Sarod	Ali Akbar Khan, Amjad Ali Khan, Alauddin Khan , Saren Rani, Brij Narayan	Ghatam	T.H. Vinayakaram
		Janjira	V. Nagarajan
		Symphony	Jubin Mehta

Wild Life Sanctuary in India

India is rich in flora and fauna. However, due to increasing population and industrial and commercial activities, there has been acute pressure on forests. The Government has taken several steps to check the sharp fall in the number of these species. Among the measures are declaration of certain habitats as national parks and sanctuaries. 104 national parks and 551 sanctuaries have been established so far, important ones being given below:

Asam: Kaziranga National Park (know for one-horn Rhinoceroses); Manas Sanctuary.

Jharkhand: Hazaribagh National Park; Betla Tiger Reserve Palamau.

Gujarat: Valvadar National Park, Bhavnagar; Marine National Park, Gir Forests.

Himachal Pradesh: Rohla National Park; Motichur Sanctuary.

Jammu & Kashmir: Dachigam Sanctuary.

Karnataka: Bandipur National Park; Bannargheta National Park, Bangalore; Nagorhole National Park, Coorg; Ranganthitto Bird Sanctuary.

Kerala: Eravikulam Rajmallay National Park, Idduki; Periyar Game Sanctuary.

Madhya Pradesh: Kanha National Park; Bandhavgarh National Park, Shahdol; Shivpuri National Park.

Maharashtra: Taloba National Park, Chandrapur; Panch National Park, Nagpur; Borivali National Park, Mumbai; Nawagaon National Park, Bandara; Melghat National Park.

Manipur: Reibul Lamjao National Park.

Odisha: Simlipal, Tiger Sanctuary.

Rajasthan: Sariska Sanctuary; Ghana Bird Sanctuary, Ranthambhor Sanctuary.

Sikkim: Khangchandzenda National Park, Gangtok.

Tamil Nadu: Vedanthangal Bird Sanctuary; Guindy National Park, Chennai; Mudumalai Sanctuary; Kalakad-Munden Thurai Reserve.

Uttar Pradesh: Chandraprabha Sanctuary; Dudhwa National Park, Lakhimpur.

West Bengal: Jaldapara Sanctuary; Sunderbans.

Uttarakhand: Corbett National Park; Nainital

Abbreviations

A

ABC	Atomic, Biological and Chemical (Warfare)
ABM	Anti-Ballistic Missile
ACC	Auxiliary Cadet Corpse
ACD	Asian Co-operation Dialogue
AD	Anno Domini (in the year of Our Lord)
ADB	Asian Development Bank
AEC	Atomic Energy Commission
AFSPA	Armed Forces Special Power Act
AICC	All India Congress Committee
AIDS	Acquired Immune Deficiency Syndrome
AIIMS	All India Institute of Medical Sciences
AITUC	All India Trade Union Congress
AMP	Auto Mission Plan
ANC	African National Congress
APPLE	Ariane Passenger Payload Experiment
ARC	Administrative Reforms Commission
ASEAN	Association for South East Asian Nations
ASI	Archaeological Survey of India
ASLV	Augmented Satellite Launch Vehicle
ASSOCHAM	Associated Chamber of Commerce and Industry
ATM	Automated Teller Machine

B

BA	Bachelor of Arts, British Academy
BARC	Bhabha Atomic Research Centre
BBC	British Broadcasting Corporation
BC	Before Christ
BCG	Bacillus Calmette Guerim (Anti-TB Vaccine)
BCCI	Board of Control for Cricket in India
BHEL	Bharat Heavy Electricals Limited
BRAI	Broadcast Regulatory Authority of India
BSF	Border Security Force
BSNL	Bharat Sanchar Nigam Limited

C

CA	Chartered Accountant
CAC	Consumer Access Codes
CBI	Central Bureau of Investigation
CBSE	Central Board of Secondary Education
CBDT	Central Board of Direct Taxes
CDMA	Code Division Multiple Axis
CDS	Compulsory Deposit Scheme
CISF	Central Industrial Security Force
CID	Criminal Investigation Department
COCA	Control of Organised Crime Act
CPCB	Central Pollution Control Board
CRPF	Central Reserve Police Force
CRR	Cash Reserve Ratio

(R-1641) GK–5

CSIR	Council of Scientific & Industrial Research
CVR	Cockpit Voice Recorder
CVC	Central Vigilance Commission

D

DGCA	Director General of Civil Aviation
DIG	Deputy Inspector General
DNA	Deoxy-ribo Nucleic Acid
DOD	Department of Ocean Development
DRDO	Defence Research Development Organisation
DSIDC	Defence Scientific Information and Documentation

E

ECG	Electro Cardiogram
ECO	Economic Cooperation Organisation
ECOSOC	Economic and Social Council (UN)
EDUSAT	Education Sattelite
EEC	European Economic Commission
EMS	European Monetary System
ESI	Employees State Insurance
ESRO	European Space Research Organisation

F

FAO	Food and Agriculture Organisation
FBI	Federal Bureau of Investigation
FERA	Foreign Exchange Regulation Act
FERB	Foreign Exchange Regulatory Board
FICCI	Federation of Indian Chambers of Commerce and Industry

G

GAIL	Gas Authority of India Limited
GATT	General Agreement on Tariffs and Trade
GMT	Greenwich Mean Time
GNP	Gross National Product
GPRS	General Packet Radio Service
GSLV	Geo-Satellite Launch Vehicle

GSM	Global System for Mobile Communications
GST	Goods and Services Tax

H

HAL	Hindustan Aeronautics Limited
HDC	Hill Development Council
HEC	Heavy Engineering Corporation
HUDCO	Housing and Urban Development Corporation

I

IAA	International Airports Authority
IA	Indian Airlines
IAF	Indian Air Force
IARI	Indian Agricultural Research Institute
IAS	Indian Administrative Service
IBM	International Business Machines
ICC	International Cricket Council
ICICI	Industrial Credit and Investment Corporation of India
ICMR	Indian Council of Medical Research
ICS	Indian Civil Service
ICWA	Indian Council of World Affairs
IDA	International Development Agency
IDBI	Industrial Development Bank of India
IFFI	International Film Festival of India
IFS	Indian Foreign Service
IGNOU	Indira Gandhi National Open University
IIT	Indian Institute of Technology
ILO	International Labour Organisation
INTELSAT	International Telecommunication Satellite
INTERPOL	International Police Organisation
INTUC	Indian National Trade Union Congress
IOC	Indian Oil Corporation
IPL	Indian Premier League
ISD	International Subscriber Dialling

(R-1641) GK–5-II

ISRO	Indian Space Research Organisation		**NASDAQ**	National Association of Securities Dealers Automated Quotation
ISI	Indian Standard Institution		**NATO**	North Atlantic Treaty Organisation
IST	Indian Standard Time		**NCC**	National Cadet Corpse
ITI	Indian Telephone Industries; Industrial Training Institute		**NCERT**	National Council of Educational Research and Training
ITO	International Trade Organisation		**NCST**	National Committee of Science and Technology
ITUC	Indian Trade Union Congress		**NDA**	National Defence Academy

J

JCO	Junior Commissioned Officer
JKLF	Jammu and Kashmir Liberation Front
JMM	Jharkhand Mukti Morcha
JPC	Joint Parliamentary Committee

K

KMT	Kuomintang (Nationalist Party of Taiwan)
KANU	Kenya African National Union

L

LASER	Light Amplification by Stimulated Emission of Radiation
LCA	Light Combat Aircraft
LIC	Life Insurance Corporation
LPG	Liquified Petroleum Gas

M

MBA	Master of Business Administration
MBBS	Bachelor of Medicine and Bachelor of Surgery
MCC	Maoits Communist Centre
MI	Military Intelligence
MLA	Member of Legislative Assembly
MNC	Multi-National Company
MODVAT	Modified Value Added Tax

N

NABARD	National Bank for Agriculture and Rural Development
NASA	National Aeronautics and Space Administration (USA)

NDRI	National Dairy Research Institute
NHAI	National Highway Authority of India
NHRC	National Human Rights Commission
NMD	National Missile Defence

O

OAPEC	Organisation of Arab Petroleum Exporting Countries
OCS	Overseas Communication Service
OPEC	Organisation of Petroleum Exporting Countries

P

PA	Personal Assistant, Press Association
PAN	Permanent Account Number
PERDA	Pension Fund Regulatory and Development Authority
POTA	Prevention of Terrorism Act
PWG	Peoples War Group

Q

QMG	Quarter Master General
QMT	Quantitative Management Technique

R

RADAR	Radio Detecting and Ranging
RAF	Rapid Action Force
RAW	Research & Analysis Wing
RBI	Reserve Bank of India
RCC	Reinforced Cement Concrete

(S)

SAARC	South Asian Association for Regional Cooperation
SAHR	South Asian for Human Rights
SAFTA	South Asian Free Trade Agreement
SALT	Strategic Arms Limitations Talks
SC	Supreme Court, Scheduled Caste
SCRA	Special Class Railway Apprentices
SEBI	Securities and Exchange Board of India
SEZ	Special Economic Zone
SEATO	South-East Asia Treaty Organisation
SHO	Station House Officer
SIM	Subscriber Identification Module

(T)

TAR	Trans Asian Railways
TISCO	Tata Iron and Steel Company
TMO	Telegraphic Money Order
TRAI	Telecom Regulatory Authority of India
TRYSEM	Training of Rural Youth for Self Employment

(U)

UTI	Unit Trust of India
UNESCO	United Nations Educational Scientific and Cultural Organisation
UNFPA	United Nations Fund for Population Activities
UNHCR	United Nations High Commission for Refugees
UNICEF	United Nations International Children's Emergency Fund
UNFCC	United Nations Framework Convention on Climate Change.

(V)

VAT	Value Added Tax
VC	Vice-Chancellor
VDIS	Voluntary Disclosure Income Scheme
VHP	Vishwa Hindu Parishad
VIP	Very Important Person
VPP	Value Payable Post
URS	Voluntary Retirement Scheme

(W)

WEF	World Environment Forum
wef	with effect from
WHO	World Health Organisation
WFP	World Food Programme
WWF	World Wild-Life Fund
WTO	World Trade Organisation
WWW	World Wide Wave

(Z)

ZETA	Zero Energy Thermal-nuclear Assembly or Apparatus
ZIP	Zonal Improvement Plan
ZPG	Zero Population Growth

Awards

National Awards

1. **Bharat Ratna:** This is India's highest civilian award. It is given for exceptional work on art, literature, science and recognition of public service of the highest order. Government servants are not eligible for it. The table shows the recipients of the award:

Bharat Ratna Award Winners:

1. Dr. S. Radhakrishnan	1954	**17.** K. Kamraj	1976	**33.** M.S. Subbalakshmi	1998
2. C. Rajagopalachari	1954	**18.** Mother Teresa	1980	**34.** C. Subramaniam	1998
3. Dr. C.V. Raman	1954	**19.** Acharya Vinoba Bhave	1983	**35.** Jaya Prakash Narayan	1999
4. Dr. Bhagwan Das	1955	**20.** Khan Abdul Ghaffar Khan	1987	**36.** Prof. Amartya Sen	1999
5. Dr. M. Visvesvaraya	1955	**21.** M.G. Ramachandran	1988	**37.** Pt. Ravi Shankar	1999
6. Jawahar Lal Nehru	1955	**22.** Dr. B.R. Ambedkar	1990	**38.** Gopinath Bardoloi	1999
7. Govind Ballabh Pant	1957	**23.** Dr. Nelson R. Mandela	1990	**39.** Lata Mangeshkar	2001
8. Dr. D.K. Karve	1958	**24.** Rajiv Gandhi	1991	**40.** Bismillah Khan	2001
9. Dr. Bidhan Chandra Roy	1961	**25.** Sardar Vallabhbhai Patel	1991	**41.** Bhimsen Joshi	2009
10. Purushottam Das Tandon	1961	**26.** Morarji R. Desai	1991	**42.** C.N.R. Rao	2014
11. Dr. Rajendra Prasad	1962	**27.** Maulana Abul Kalam Azad	1992	**43.** Sachin Tendulkar	2014
12. Dr. Zakir Hussain	1963	**28.** Jehangir Ratanji Dadabhai Tata	1992	**44.** Madan Mohan Malaviya	2015
13. Dr. Pandurang Vaman Kane	1963	**29.** Satyajit Roy	1992	**45.** Atal Bihari Vajpayee	2015
14. Lal Bahadur Shastri	1966	**30.** Shri Gulzari Lal Nanda	1997	**46.** Nanaji Deshmukh	2019
15. Indira Gandhi	1971	**31.** Mrs. Aruna Asaf Ali	1997	**47.** Bhupen Hazarika	2019
16. V.V. Giri	1975	**32.** Dr. A.P.J. Abdul Kalam	1997	**48.** Pranab Mukherjee	2019

2. **Padma Vibhushan:** This award is given for exceptional and distinguished service in any field, including service rendered by Govt. servants.
3. **Padma Bhushan:** This award is given for distinguished service of a high order in any field, including service rendered by Govt. servants.
4. **Padma Shri:** This award is given for distinguished service in any field, including service rendered by Government servants.

Gallantry Awards

1. **Param Vir Chakra:** The highest award for bravery or some daring and pre-eminent act of valour or self-sacrifice in the presence of the enemy, whether on land, at sea or in the air.
2. **Mahavir Chakra:** It is the second highest decoration and is awarded for acts of conspicuous gallantry in the presence of the enemy, whether on land, at sea or in the air.
3. **Vir Chakra:** It is the third in order of awards given for acts of gallantry in the presence of enemy, whether on land, at sea or in the air.
4. **Ashok Chakra:** This medal is awarded for the most conspicuous bravery or some daring or pre-eminent act of valour or self-sacrifice on land, at sea or in the air but not in the presence of enemy.

5. **Vishishta Sewa Medal:** It is awarded to personnel of all the three Services in class I, II and III in recognition of distinguished service of the "most exceptional" and "exceptional" and a "high" order respectively. Prefixes *Parma* and *Ati* are added before first two categories of medals respectively.

6. **Jeewan Raksha Padak:** Awarded for meritorious acts or a series of acts of a human nature displayed in saving life from drowning, fire and rescue operations in mines etc.

Other National Awards

1. **Krishi Pandit:** This title is awarded annually by the Indian Council of Agriculture Research to farmers for their special contribution.

2. **National Sports Awards 2018: Rajiv Gandhi Khel Ratna Award:** Mirabai Chanu (Weightlifting), Virat Kohli (Cricket). **Arjuna Award:** Neeraj Chopra (Athletics), Subedar Jinson Johnson (Athletics), Hima Das (Athletics), Nelakurthi Sikki Reddy (Badminton), Subedar Satish Kumar (Boxing), Smriti Mandhana (Cricket), Shubhankar Sharma (Golf), Manpreet Singh (Hockey), Savita (Hockey), Col. Ravi Rathore (Polo), Rahi Sarnobat (Shooting), Ankur Mittal (Shooting), Shreyasi Singh (Shooting), Manika Batra (Table Tennis), G. Sathiyan (Table Tennis), Rohan Bopanna (Tennis), Sumit (Wrestling), Pooja Kadian (Wushu), Ankur Dhama (Para-Athletics) and Manoj Sarkar (Para-Badminton). **Dronacharya Awards:** Subedar Chenanda Achaiah Kuttappa (Boxing), Vijay Sharma (Weightlifting), A. Srinivasa Rao (Table Tennis), Sukhdev Singh Pannu (Athletics), Clarence Lobo (Hockey), Tarak Sinha (Cricket), Jiwan Kumar Sharma (Judo) and V.R. Beedu (Athletics). **Dhyanchand Awards:** Satyadev Prasad (Archery), Bharat Kumar Chetri (Hockey), Bobby Aloysius (Athletics) and Chougale Dadu Dattatray (Wrestling).

3. **Sahitya Akademi Awards:** These prizes are awarded annually to the authors of the most outstanding books of literary merit published in each of the 22 languages recognised by the Akademi. There are also two awards for Sanskrit and English. The award, inform of a casket containing an inscribed copper plate and a cheque of ₹ 1 lakh is given to the author or his/her heir.

4. **Dada Saheb Phalke Award:** The award carries a cash prize of ₹ 10 lakh, a Shawl and Swarna Kamal. Recipients of Dada Saheb Phalke Award are:

Dada Saheb Phalke Award Winners:

Mrs Devika Rani Roerich	1969	Raj Kapoor	1987	Yash Chopra	2001
		Ashok Kumar	1988	Devanand	2002
B.N. Sirkar	1970	Lata Mangeshkar	1989	Mrinal Sen	2003
Prithvi Raj Kapoor	1971	A. Nageshwar Rao	1990	Adur Gopala Krishnan	2004
Pankaj Mallick	1972	Bhalji Pendharkar	1991		
Mrs Ruby Myers	1973	Bhupen Hazarika	1992	Shyam Benegal	2005
B.N. Reddy	1974	Majrooh Sultanpuri	1993	Tapan Sinha	2006
Dhiren Ganguly	1975	Dilip Kumar	1994	Manna Dey	2007
Mrs Kanan Devi	1976	Dr Raj Kumar (Kannada actor)	1995	V.K. Murthy	2008
Nitin Bose	1977			D. Ramanaidu	2009
R.C. Boral	1978	Sivaji Ganesan (Tamil Actor)	1996	K. Balachander	2010
Sohrab Modi	1979			Soumitra Chatterjee	2011
P. Jai Raj	1980	Pradeepji (Poet, lyricist)	1997	Pran	2012
Naushad Ali	1981			Gulzar	2013
L.V. Prasad	1982	B.R. Chopra	1998	Shashi Kapoor	2014
Mrs. Durga Khote	1983	Hrishikesh Mukherjee	1999	Manoj Kumar	2015
Satyajit Roy	1984			K. Viswanath	2016
V. Shantaram	1985	Asha Bhonsle (Playback singer)	2000	Vinod Khanna	2017
B. Nagi Reddy	1986				

5. **Jnanpith Award 2018:** Eminent English writer Amitav Ghosh has been selected for the prestigious Jnanpith Award-2018 for his contribution to the enrichment of English literature through his creative writing.

6. **65th National Film Awards-2017:** Regional cinema dominated the 65th National Film Awards announced on April 13, 2018. Assamese film *Village Rockstars* won the award in the Best Feature Film category. *Baahubali 2: The Conclusion directed by S.S. Rajamouli* was selected as the Best Popular Film providing wholesome entertainment. Awards in various categories are as follows: ***Best Feature Film:*** *Village Rockstars* (Assamese); ***Best Director:*** *Jayaraj* (Bhayanakam—Malayalam); ***Best Actress:*** *Sridevi* (Mom); ***Best Actor:*** *Riddhi Sen* (Nagar Kirtan); ***Best Choreography:*** *Ganesh Acharya* (Toilet Ek Prem Katha); ***Special Jury Award:*** *Nagar Kirtan* (Bengali); ***Best Lyrics:*** Muthurathinam; ***Best Music Direction:*** *A.R. Rahman* (Kaatru Veliyidayi); ***Best Screenplay Original:*** Thondimuthalum Driksakshiyum; ***Best Screenplay Adapted:*** Bhayanakam; ***Best Cinematography:*** Bhayanakam; ***Best Female Playback Singer:*** *Sasha Tirupati* (Kaatru Veliyidayi); ***Best Male Playback Singer:*** *K.J. Yesudas* (Poy Maranja Kalam from Viswasapoorvam Mansoor); ***Best Children's Film:*** Mhorkya; ***Best Film on Environmental Conservation:*** Irada; ***Best Feature Film on National Integration:*** *Dhappa* (Marathi); ***Best Debut Film of Director:*** Sinjar; ***Best Popular Film Providing Wholesome Entertainment:*** *Baahubali 2: The Conclusion.*

7. **Dayawati Modi Award:** The Dayawati Modi Award for Art, Culture and Education is presented annually to an eminent person credited with outstanding contributions in these fields.

8. **National Science Award:** Instituted on the first National Science Day, observed on February 28, 1987. The award for outstanding contribution in popularising science among people carries a cash prize of ₹ 1 lakh.

9. **Saraswati Samman 2018:** Given for outstanding literary works, value ₹ 15 lakh. The award for the year 2018 has been given to Telugu poet K. Siva Reddy for his collection of poems titled Pakkaki Ottigilite.

10. **Best Parliamentarian Award:** The Best Parliament Member Award for 2015, 2016 and 2017 have been conferred on Gulam Nabi Azad (Congress), Dinesh Trivedi (TMC) and Bhartruhari Mahtab (BJD) respectively.

11. **Kalinga Prize:** This award is given each year by the UNESCO and founded by former Odisha Chief Minister late Shri Biju Patnaik for popularisation of science.

12. **Jamnalal Bajaj Awards 2018:** Each of the award comprises a cash prize of ₹ 10 lakh, a trophy and citation. It is given for outstanding role in different walks of life. The winners of 2018 award are Mr. Dhoom Singh Negi, Ms. Rupal Desai & Mr. Rajendra Desai, Ms. Prasanna Bhandari and Dr. Clayborne Carson.

13. **Vyas Samman 2018:** This is awarded by KK Birla Foundation for outstanding Hindi Literary work by an Indian citizen that was published in the past decade. This carries a cash prize of ₹ 4.0 lakh. The award for 2018 has been given to Noted Hindi writer Leeladhar Jagudi for his collection of poems "Jitne Log Utne Prem"

International Awards

1. **Nobel Prizes:** These Prizes were instituted in 1901 by a Swedish scientist, Dr. Alfred Nobel; the discoverer of Dynamite. Six prizes are awarded annually for (i) Chemistry, (ii) Physics, (iii) Medicine, (iv) Literature, (v) Peace and (vi) Economics — started since 1969. The following Indians so far have been awarded these prizes: (i) Dr. Rabindra Nath Tagore (1913) for his *"Geetanjali".* (ii) Dr. C.V. Raman for Physics in 1930, (iii) Mother Teresa for Peace in 1979, (iv) Prof. Amartya Sen in 1998 for Economics and (v) Kailash Styarthi for Peace in 2014.

Nobel Prize 2018: *Physics:* Arthur Ashkin (96) of USA, Gerard Mourou (74) of France and Donna Strickland (59) of Canada "for groundbreaking inventions in the field of laser physics. *Chemistry:* American scientists Frances H. Arnold and George P. Smith and British researcher Gregory P. Winter "for applying the principles of evolution to develop enzymes used to make everything from biofuels to medicine". *Physiology or Medicine:* James P. Allison of the USA and Tasuku Honjo of Japan "for game-changing discoveries about how to harness and manipulate the immune system to fight cancer". *Literature:* The Nobel Prize in Literature will not be handed out this year after the awarding body was hit by a sexual misconduct scandal. *Peace:* Denis Mukwege, a doctor who helps victims of sexual violence in the Democratic Republic of Congo, and Nadia Murad, a Yazidi rights activist in northern Iraq and survivor of sexual slavery by the Islamic State "for their efforts to end the use of sexual violence as a weapon of war and armed conflicts". *Economic Sciences:* US economists William Nordhaus and Paul Romer "for constructing 'green growth' models that show how innovation and climate policies can be integrated with economic growth".

2. **Magsaysay Awards-2018:** The 2018 awardees are: ● **Youk Chhang *(Cambodia)*** for his great leadership and vision in transforming the memory of horror into a process of attaining and preserving justice in his nation and the world; ● **Maria de Lourdes Martins Cruz *(East Timor)*** for her pure humanitarianism in uplifting Timor Leste's poor and her valiant pursuit of social justice and peace; ● **Howard Dee *(The Philippines)*** for his abiding dedication to the pursuit of social justice and peace in achieving dignity and progress for the poor; ● **Bharat Vatwani *(India)*** for his tremendous courage and healing compassion in embracing India's mentally-afflicted destitute; ● **Vo Thi Hoang Yen *(Vietnam)*** for her creative, charismatic leadership in the sustained campaign to break down physical and mental barriers that have marginalized PWDs in Vietnam; ● **Sonam Wangchuk *(India)*** for his uniquely systematic, collaborative and community-driven reform of learning systems in remote northern India especially Ladakh.

3. **Gandhi Peace Prize:** The government instituted this ₹ 1 crore prize on the lines of the Nobel Peace Prize in 1995. It is the highest Civilian International award by the Govt. of India. The winner of 2018 is Yohei Sasakawa, the goodwill ambassador of the WHO.

4. **Man Booker Prize 2018:** Author Anna Burns has become the first Northern Irish writer, and the first woman since 2013, to win Britain's renowned Man Booker Prize for her novel *Milkman.* Judges of the annual award praised the work, an exploration of Northern Ireland's three decades of sectarian violence told through the voice of a young woman, as "utterly distinctive". The 56-year-old is the first woman in five years to land the most prestigious English-language literary prize, after Eleanor Catton became the youngest winner, at the age of 28, in 2013.

5. **Indira Gandhi Prize for Peace, Disarmament and Development:** The award was instituted in the memory of Mrs. Indira Gandhi to foster creative cooperation among nations of the world. The award for 2018 has been given to Delhi based environment think tank CSE. This prize carries ₹ 25 lakh and a citation.

91st Oscar Award (Declared in 2019)

The grand ceremony of the 91st Academy Awards or Oscar Awards was held on February 24, 2019 in Los Angeles, California. The winners are: *Best Picture:* Green Book; *Best Actor:* Rami Malek *(Bohemian Rhapsody)*; *Best Actress:* Olivia Colman *(The Favourite)*; *Best Director:* Alfonso Cuaron *(Roma)*; *Best Supporting Actor:* Mahershala Ali *(Green Book)*; *Best Supporting Actress:* Regina King *(If Beale Street Could Talk)*; *Best Original Screenplay:* Green Book; *Best Adapted Screenplay:* BlacKkKlansman; *Best Animated Film:* Spider-Man: Into the Spider-Verse; *Best Foreign Language Film:* Roma; *Best Documentary Film:* Free Solo; *Best Original Song:* Shallow *(A Star is Born)*.

Miss World-2018

This competition was established in 1951 by the 'Miss World Incorporation'. The winner of 2018 is Vanessa Ponce de Leon of Mexico. Nicolene Pichapa Limsnukan of Thailand was first runner-up and Maria Vasilevich of Belarus second runner up.

BAFTA Awards 2019

The British Academy of Film and Television Arts (Bafta) awards were handed out in London on February 10, 2019. The winners are: ● **Film:** Roma; ● **Outstanding British Film:** The Favourite; ● **Director:** Alfonso Cuaron, (Roma); ● **Original screenply:** Deborah Davis, Tony McNamara, (The Favourite); ● **Leading Actor:** Rami Malek (Bohemian Rhapsody); ● **Leading Actress:** Olivia Colman (The Favourite); ● **Supporting Actor:** Mahershala Ali (Green Book); ● **Supporting Actress:** Rachel Weisz (The Favourite); ● **Orignal Music:** Bradley Cooper, Lady Gaga, Lukas Nelson (A Star is Born); ● **Cinema-tography:** Alfonso Cuaron (Roma); ● **Editing:** Hank Corwin (Vice); ● **Production Design:** Fiona Crombie, Alice Felton (The Favourite).

Miss Universe-2018

The 67th Miss Universe pageant was held on 17 December 2018 at Thailand. Demi-Leigh Nel-Peters of South Africa crowned her successor Catriona Gray of the Philippines at the end of the event. Tamaryn Green of South Africa and Sthefany Gutierrez of Venezuela were adjudged the first and second runner-up respectively.

Jawaharlal Nehru Award for International Understanding

This award was instituted in 1964 by the Indian Council of Cultural Relations to be awarded to a person who contributed the most to the understanding and friendship between different countries. The first J.L. Nehru Award was given in 1965 to U. Thant (3rd U.N.O. Secretary General). In 1995, it was given to Hosni Mubarak (President of Egypt). *2006:* Lula da Silva (President of Brazil); *2007:* Dr. Olafer Ragnar Grimson (President of Republic of Iceland). **2008:** No Award; **2009:** Angela Merkel (Chancellor of Germany) (No award has been given since 2010).

Pulitzer Prize, 2019

Aretha Franklin received an honorary Pulitzer Prize on April 15, 2019, as judges praised the Queen of Soul for her indelible contribution to American music and culture. David W. Blight's 900-page Frederick Douglass was named the best work of history, while the biography prize went to Jeffrey C. Stewart's *The New Negro: The Life of Alain Locke*. Richard Powers' innovative novel The Overstory, which shows us the world through the perspective of nature, won for fiction. The drama prize went to Fairview, by Jackie Sibblies Drury and Eliza Griswold's *Amity and Prosperity : One Family and the Fracturing of America* won for general nonfiction. Ellen Reid's opera 'prism', which tackles sexual and emotional abuse, was given the music award. The *New York Times* and *The Wall Street Journal* won prizes for their separate investigations on US President Donald Trump and his family.

61st Grammy Awards, 2019

The 61st Grammy Awards honouring the best in the music industry were presented at a ceremony in Los Angeles on February 10, 2019. The winners are: ● **Album of the Year:** Golden Hour (Kacey Musgraves); ● **Record of the Year:** This is America (Childish Gambino); ● **Song of the Year:** This is America (Childish Gambino); ● **Best New Artist:** Dua Lipa; ● **Best Pop Solo Performance:** Lady Gaga, Joanne (Whre Do You Think You're Goin?); ● **Best Pop Duo/Group Performance:** Lady Gaga and Bradley Cooper (Shallow); ● **Best Country Album:** Kacey Musgraves (Golden Hour); ● **Best Pop Vocal Album:** Ariana Grande (Sweetener); ● **Best Traditional Pop Vocal Album:** Willie Nelson (My Way) ● **Best Rap Performance:** Kendrick Lamar, Jay Rock, Future & James Blake (King's Dead), Anderson Paak (Bubblin); ● **Best Rap/Sung Collaboration:** Childish Gambino (This is America); ● **Best Rap Song:** Drake (God's Plan); ● **Best Rap Album:** Cardi B. Invasion of Privacy; ● **Best Rock Performance:** Chris Cornell (When Bad Does Good); ● **Best Metal Performance:** High on Fire (Electric Messiah); ● **Best Rock Song:** St. Vincent (Masseduction); ● **Best Alternative Music Album:** Arctic Monkeys (Tranquility Base Hotel & Casino); ● **Best Rock Album:** Greta Van Fleet (From the Fires).

Highest Honours of Some Countries

Country	Highest Honour	Country	Highest Honour
India	Bharat Ratna	Britain	Member of British Empire, Victoria Cross
Pakistan	Nishan-e-Pakistan		
Kuwait	Mubarak-Al-kabir Medal	Japan	Order of Moulovenice Sun
Saudi Arabia	Shah Abdul Aziz Medal		
Argentina	The Order of Sona Martin	Denmark	Order of Diana Brog
Nicaragua	Augusto-Caesar Sandino Order	France	Legend of Honour
		America	Presidential Medal of Freedom
Vietnam	The order of the Golden Star		
		Germany	Pore Lee Merit Iron Cross
Hungary	The Order of Banner	The Netherlands	Netherlands Lion

76th Golden Globe Awards 2019

The 76th Golden Globe Awards ceremony was held in Los Angeles on January 6, 2019. Freddie Mercury biopic Bohemian Rhapsody pulled a major upset at the close of the ceremony, taking home the final two top prizes—Best Drama & Best Actor—to put itself into the Oscar conversation along with Green Book and Roma. Main awardees are: **FILMS:** ● **Best Film (Drama):** Bohemian Rhapsody, ● **Best Director:** Alfonso Cuaron (Roma), ● **Best Actor (Drama):** Rami Malek (Bohemian Rhapsody), ● **Best Actress (Drama):** Glenn Close (The Wife), ● **Best Supporting Actor:** Mahershala Ali (Green Book), ● **Best Supporting Actress:** Regina King (If Beale Street Could Talk), ● **Best Film (Comedy or Musical):** Green Book, ● **Best Actor (Comedy or Musical):** Christian Bale (Vice), ● **Best Actress (Comedy or Musical):** Olivia Colman (The Favourite), ● **Best Film (Animated):** Spider-Man : Into the Spider-Verse, ● **Best Film (Foreign Language):** Roma (Mexico). **TELEVISION:** ● **Best Drama Series:** The Americans, ● **Best Actor (Drama):** Richard Madden (Bodyguard), ● **Best Actress (Drama):** Sandra Oh (Killing Eve), ● **Best Musical or Comedy Series:** The Kominsky Method, ● **Best Actor (Comedy or Musical):** Michael Douglas (The Kominsky Method), ● **Best Actress (Comedy or Musical):** Rachel Brosnahan (The Marvelous Mrs. Maisel).

❑❑❑

Sports

Important Cups & Trophies

International

• *American Cup*	: Yacht Racing	• *U. Thant Cup*	: Tennis
• *Ashes*	: Cricket	• *Walker Cup*	: Golf
• *Benson and Hedges*	: Cricket	• *Westchester Cup*	: Polo
• *Canada Cup*	: Golf	• *Wightman Cup*	: Lawn Tennis
• *Colombo Cup*	: Football	• *World Cup*	: Cricket
• *Corbitton Cup*	: Table Tennis (Women)	• *World Cup*	: Hockey
• *Davis Cup*	: Lawn Tennis	• *Reliance Cup*	: Cricket
• *Derby*	: Horse Race	• *Rothman's Trophy*	: Cricket
• *Grand National*	: Horse Streple Chase Race	• *William's Cup*	: Basketball
		• *European Champions Cup*	: Football
• *Jules Rimet Trophy*	: World Soccer Cup	• *Eisenhower Cup*	: Golf
• *King's Cup*	: Air Races	• *Essande Champions Cup*	: Hockey
• *Merdeka Cup*	: Football	• *Rene Frank Trophy*	: Hockey
• *Ryder Cup*	: Golf	• *Grand Prix*	: Table Tennis
• *Swaythling Cup*	: Table Tennis (Men)	• *Edgbaston Cup*	: Lawn Tennis
• *Thomas Cup*	: Badminton	• *Grand Prix*	: Lawn Tennis
• *Uber Cup*	: Badminton (Women)	• *World Cup*	: Weightlifting

National

• *Agarwal Cup*	: Badminton	• *C.K. Naydu Trophy*	: Cricket
• *Agha Khan Cup*	: Hockey	• *Chakola Gold Trophy*	: Football
• *All India Women's*		• *Divan Cup*	: Badminton
Guru Nanak		• *Deodhar Trophy*	: Cricket
Championship	: Hockey	• *Duleep Trophy*	: Cricket
• *Bandodkar Trophy*	: Football	• *D.C.M. Cup*	: Football
• *Bangalore Blues*		• *Durand Cup*	: Football
Challenge Cup	: Basketball	• *Dhyan Chand Trophy*	: Hockey
• *Barna-Bellack Cup*	: Table Tennis	• *Dr. B.C. Roy Trophy*	: Football (Junior)
• *Beighton Cup*	: Hockey	• *Ezra Cup*	: Polo
• *Bombay Gold Cup*	: Hockey	• *F.A. Cup*	: Football
• *Burdwan Trophy*	: Weightlifting	• *G.D. Birla Trophy*	: Cricket
• *Charminar Trophy*	: Atheletics	• *Ghulam Ahmed Trophy*	: Cricket
• *Chadha Cup*	: Badminton	• *Gurmeet Trophy*	: Hockey

• *Guru Nanak Cup*	: Hockey		• *Ranjit Singh Gold Cup*	: Hockey
• *Gyanvati Devi Trophy*	: Hockey		• *Rajendra Prasad Cup*	: Tennis
• *Holkar Trophy*	: Bridge		• *Ramanujan Trophy*	: Table Tennis
• *Irani Trophy*	: Cricket		• *Rene Frank Trophy*	: Hockey
• *I.F.A. Shield*	: Football		• *Radha Mohan Cup*	: Polo
• *Indira Gold Cup*	: Hockey		• *Raghbir Singh Memorial*	: Football
• *Jawaharlal Challenge*	: Air Racing		• *Rohinton Baria Trophy*	: Cricket
• *Jaswant Singh Trophy*	: Best Services Sportsman		• *Rovers Cup*	: Football
• *Kuppuswamy Naidu Trophy*	: Hockey		• *Sanjay Gold Cup*	: Football
• *Lady Rattan Tata Trophy*	: Hockey		• *Santosh Trophy*	: Football
• *MCC Trophy*	: Hockey		• *Sir Ashutosh Mukherjee*	: Football
• *Moinuddaula Gold Cup*	: Cricket		• *Subroto Cup*	: Football
• *Murugappa Gold Cup*	: Hockey		• *Scindia Gold Cup*	: Hockey
• *Modi Gold Cup*	: Hockey		• *Sahni Trophy*	: Hockey
• *Narang Cup*	: Badminton		• *Sheesh Mahal Trophy*	: Cricket
• *Nehru Trophy*	: Hockey		• *Todd Memorial Trophy*	: Football
• *Nixan Gold Cup*	: Football		• *Tommy Eman Gold Cup*	: Hockey
• *Obaidullah Gold Cup*	: Hockey		• *Vittal Trophy*	: Football
• *Prithi Singh Cup*	: Polo		• *Vizzy Trophy*	: Cricket
• *Rani Jhansi Trophy*	: Cricket		• *Vijay Merchant Trophy*	: Cricket
• *Ranji Trophy*	: Cricket		• *Wellington Trophy*	: Rowing
• *Rangaswami Cup*	: Hockey		• *Wills Trophy*	: Cricket

Sports Measurements

- *Badminton Courts:* 44 ft. by 20 ft. (doubles) 44 ft. by 17 ft. (singles)
- *Boxing Ring:* 12 ft. by 28 ft. Sq.
- *Cricket Pitch:* 22 yards (distance)
- *Derby Course:* 1½ miles. (2.4 km)
- *Football Field:*
  (a) Length : 100 – 120 yards.
    [Breadth: 50 – 56 yards.
- (b) Rugby : 100 yards by 75 yards
- *Hockey Ground:* 100 yards by 55 to 60 yards
- *Lawn Tennis Court:* 78 ft. by 36 ft. (double), 78 ft. by 28 ft. (single)
- *Marathon Race:* 26 miles, 385 yards
- *Polo Ground:* 300 yards by 200 yards (if boarded)
- *Golf:* Hole 4½ inches in diameter.

Sports Terms

- **Badminton:** Mixed doubles; Deuce; Drop; Smash; Let; Foot work; Setting.
- **Base Ball:** Pitcher; Put out, Strike; Home; Bunt.
- **Billiards:** Cue; Jigger; Pot; Break; In Baulk; In Off; Cannons.
- **Boxing:** Upper cut; Round; Punch; Bout; Knock down; Hitting below the belt; Ring.
- **Bridge:** Finesse; Dummy; Revoke; Grand Slam; Little Slam; No Trump; Rubber.
- **Chess:** Bishop, Gambit; Checkmate; Stalemate.
- **Cricket:** L.B.W. *(leg before wicket)*; Creases, Popping-creases; Stumped; Bye; Leg-Bye; Googly; Hattrick; Maiden over; Drive; Bowling; Duck; Follow-on; No ball; Leg Break; Silly point; Cover point; Hit-wicket; Late-cut; Slip; Off-spinner; In-swing.
- **Football:** Off Side; Block; Drop-kick; Penalty-kick (or *goal kick*); Corner-kick; Free-kick; Dribble; Thrown-in; Foul.
- **Golf:** Boggy; Foursome; Stymic; Tee; Put; Hole; Niblic; Caddie; Links; The green; Bunker.
- **Hockey:** Carried; Short Corner; Bully; Sticks; Off side; Roll in; Striking Circle; Under-cutting; Dribble.

- **Horse racing:** Jockey; Punter.
- **Polo:** Bunker; Chukker; Mallet.
- **Tennis:** Back hand drive; Volley; Smash; Half-volley; Deuce; Service; Let; Grand Slam.

Stadiums & Places Associated with Sports

Name of Stadium	Sports	Place	Name of Stadium	Sports	Place
Ferozshah Kolta Ground	Cricket	Delhi	Black Heath	Rugby Football	London
Jawaharlal Nehru Stadium	Athletics	Delhi	Henley	Boat race	England
Shivajee Stadium	Hockey	Delhi	Wimbledon	Lawn Tennis	London
National Stadium	Hockey etc.	Delhi	Wembley Stadium	Football	London
Indraprastha Stadium	Indoor Games	Delhi	Hurlingham	Polo	England
Ambedkar Stadium	Football	Delhi	White City	Dog-race	England
Brabourne Stadium	Cricket	Mumbai	Aintree	Horse-race	England
Wankhede Stadium	Cricket	Mumbai	Tentbridge	Cricket	England
National Stadium	Hockey etc.	Mumbai	Patnee Martlake	Boat-race	England
Eden Garden	Cricket	Kolkata	Tibankham	Rugby Football	England
Ranjeet Stadium	Football	Kolkata	Brookland	Football	England
Green Park Stadium	Cricket	Kanpur	Sandy Lodge	Golf	Scotland
Keenan Stadium	Cricket	Jamshedpur	Forest Hill	Tennis	New York
Nehru (Chepauk) Stadium	Cricket	Chennai	Brooklyn	Baseball	New York
Barabati Stadium	Cricket	Cuttack	Yankee Stadium	Boxing	New York
Epsum	Derby race	Britain	Perth, Brisbane,		
Lords, Oval, Leeds	Cricket	Britain	Melbourne	Cricket	Australia
Hedingle Manchester	Cricket	Britain			

Name of Playing Compound of Different Games

Name of Compound	Related Sports	Name of Compound	Related Sports
Court	Lawn Tennis, Badminton, Netball, Hand ball, Volleyball, Squash, Kho-Kho, Kabaddi	Pool	Swimming
		Alley	Bowling
		Mat	Judo, Karate II
Diamond	Baseball	Arena	Horse Riding
Ring	Boxing, Skating, Wrestling, Circus, Riding display	Vellodrum	Cycling
		Field	Polo, Football, Hockey
		Track	Athletics
Course	Golf	Pitch	Cricket, Rugby
Board	Table Tennis	Rink	Ice Hockey

National Sports and Games of Some Countries

Australia	Cricket	Scotland	Rugby Football
Canada	Ice Hockey	Spain	Bull Fighting
England	Cricket and Rugby Football	USA	Baseball
India	Hockey	China	Table Tennis
Japan	Ju-Jitsu	Malaysia	Badminton
Russia	Chess	Pakistan	Hockey

Number of Players in Some Games/Sports

Sports	No. of Players	Sports	No. of Players	Sports	No. of Players
Badminton	1 or 2	Cricket	11	Football (Rugby)	15
Baseball	9	Croquest	13 or 15	Table	1 or
Basketball	5	Football (Soccer)	11	Tennis	2
Billiards (Snooker)	1	Hockey	11	Lawn	1 or
Boxing	1	Lacrosse	12	Tennis	2
Bridge	2	Netball	7	Volleyball	6
Chess	1	Polo Rugby	4	Water Polo	7

Olympic Games

First of all these games were held by the Greeks in 776 B.C. on Mount Olympus in honour of the Greek God Zeus. In this way, the history of Olympic Games is about twenty eight hundred years old. These games continued to be held every four years until 394 A.D. When these games were stopped by a royal order of the emperor of Rome. The modern Olympic Games which started in Athens in 1896, are the result of the devotion and dedication of a French educator Baron Pierre de Coubertin and the first Olympic meet in the modern series was held in 1896 in Athens, the Capital of Greece. Since then, they are being held every four years except for breaks during world wars. The Olympic flag is white in colour with five coloured rings, each ring symbolic of a continent. Summer as well as winter Olympics are held in the same year.

Olympic Games (Venues & Dates)

Year	Venue	Organising	Participating Countries	Year	Venue	Organising	Participating Countries
1896	Athens	6–15 April	13	1960	Rome	25th August to 11th September	83
1900	Paris	20th May to 28th October	22	1964	Tokyo	10th to 24th October	93
1904	St. Louis	1st July to 23rd November	13	1968	Mexico City	12th to 27th October	112
1908	London	27th April to 31st October	22	1972	Munich	26th August to 10 September	122
1912	Stockholm	5th May to 22nd July	28	1976	Montreal	17th July to 1st September	88
1916	Berlin	Cancelled due to World War	—	1980	Moscow	19th July to 3rd Aug.	81
1920	Antwerp	20th April to 12th September	29	1984	Los Angeles	28th July to 12th August	140
1924	Paris	4th May to 27th July	44	1988	Seoul	17th September to 2nd October	160
1928	Amsterdam	17th May to 12 Aug.	46	1992	Barcelona	25th July to 9th Aug.	170
1932	Los Angeles	30th July to 14th Aug.	47	1996	Atlanta	19th July to 4th Aug.	197
1936	Berlin	1st May to 16th Aug.	49	2000	Sydney	15th September to 1st October	199
1940	Tokyo (Helsinki)	Cancelled due to Wold War	—	2004	Athens	14th to 29th August	202
1944	London	Cancelled due to World War	—	2008	Beijing	8th to 24th August	204
1948	London	29th July to 14th Aug.	59	2012	London	27th July to 12 August	204
1952	Helsinki	19th July to 3rd Aug.	69	2016	Rio de Janeiro	5th to 21st August	207
1956	Melbourne	22nd November to 8th December	71	2020	Tokyo	(to be held)	

Note: Games not held in 1916, 1940, and 1944.

Asian Games

After the Second World War, most of the Asian Countries gained independence. On the lines of Olympic Games, Asian Games were planned every four years. India hosted the first Asian Games in 1951.

Asian Games: An Overview

Year	Venues	Participating Countries	No. of Games	First Position	Year	Venues	Participating Countries	No. of Games	First Position
1951	New Delhi	11	6	Japan	1986	Seoul	34	25	China
1954	Manila	18	7	Japan	1990	Beijing	37	27	China
1958	Tokyo	20	13	Japan	1994	Hiroshima	42	34	China
1962	Jakarta	16	13	Japan	1998	Bangkok	41	36	China
1966	Bangkok	18	14	Japan	2002	Busan	44	38	China
1970	Bangkok	18	13	Japan	2006	Doha	46	43	China
1974	Teheran	25	16	Japan	2010	Guangzhou	45	42	China
1978	Bangkok	25	19	Japan	2014	Incheon	45	36	China
1982	New Delhi	33	21	China	2018	Jakarta	45	40	China
					2022	Hangzhou (China) Scheduled			

Commonwealth Games

The Commonwealth Games are held every four years, in the year in which Asian Games are held. All the Commonwealth Countries (former colonies of Britain) can take part in it. The first Commonwealth Games were held in 1930 at Hamilton (Canada).

Venues of Commonwealth Games

Venues	Year	Countries	Events	Venues	Year	Countries	Events
Hamilton,(Canada)	1930	11	6	Brisbane, (Australia)	1982	47	10
London, (U.K.)	1934	16	6	Edinburgh, (U.K.)	1986	26	10
Sydney,(Australia)	1938	15	7	Auckland, (New Zealand)	1990	55	10
Auckland, (New Zealand)	1950	12	7	Victoria, (Canada)	1994	64	
Vancouver, (Canada)	1954	24	9	Kuala Lumpur, (Malaysia)	1998	70	16
Cardiff, (U.K.)	1958	35	9	Manchester, (U.K.)	2002	72	17
Perth, (Australia)	1962	35	9	Melbourne, (Australia)	2006	71	16
Jamaica, (West Indies)	1966	34	9	Delhi, (India)	2010	71	17
Edinburgh, (U.K.)	1970	42	9	Glasgow, (Scotland)	2014	71	17
Christchurch, (NZ)	1974	39	9	Gold Coast (Aus.)	2018	71	17
Edmonton, (Canada)	1978	48	10	Birmingham (U.K.)	2022	(Scheduled)	

World Cup Football

Year	Winner	Runners-Up	Year	Winner	Runners-Up
1930	Uruguay	Argentina	1982	Italy	W. Germany
1934	Italy	Czechoslovakia	1986	Argentina	W. Germany
1938	Italy	Hungary	1990	W. Germany	Argentina
1950	Uruguay	Brazil	1994	Brazil	Italy
1954	W. Germany	Hungary	1998	France	Brazil
1958	Brazil	Sweden	2002	Brazil	Germany
1962	Brazil	Czechoslovakia	2006	Italy	France
1966	England	West Germany	2010	Spain	Netherlands
1970	Brazil	Italy	2014	Germany	Argentina
1974	W. Germany	Netherland	2018	France	Croatia
1978	Argentina	Netherland	2022	Qatar (Scheduled)	

World Cup Cricket

Year	Venue	Winner/Runner
1975	U.K.	West Indies beat Australia
1979	U.K.	West Indies beat England
1983	U.K.	India beat West Indies
1987	India & Pakistan	Australia beat England
1992	Australia	Pakistan beat England
1996	India, Pakistan & Sri Lanka	Sri Lanka beat Australia
1999	U.K.	Australia beat Pakistan
2003	South Africa	Australia beat India
2007	West Indies	Australia beat Sri Lanka
2011	India, Sri Lanka, Bangladesh	India beat Sri Lanka
2015	Australia, New Zealand	Australia beat New Zealand
2019	England	England beat New Zealand
2023	India	(to be held)

ICC CRICKET WORLD CUP 2019: In one of the most dramatic World Cup finals ever, England won the title for the first time on July 14, 2019 at Lords in London in their fourth time in a title clash. The English team had lost to West Indies at Lord's in 1979. Australia at Eden Gardens in 1987 and Pakistan in the MCG in 1992. England won after a super over after the scores ended tied after 50 overs each. The 2015 World Cup runners-up New Zealand batting first scored 241 for eight. In reply England also scored 241 for ten and the final advanced to super over. This was the first time a World Cup Final was decided with a super over. Both teams scored 15 runs in their super overs, but England lifted the trophy due to a tie-break rule because they hit the most boundaries. With this win England became the sixth country after West Indies, Australia, India, Sri Lanka and Pakistan to win the ICC Cricket World Cup.

Before the title class New Zealand beat India in the 1st Semi-Final at Old Trafford on July 10 and England beat Australia at Edgbaston on July 11 in the second Semi-Final.

ASIAN GAMES 2018: The 2018 Asian Games (Indonesian : Pesta Olahraga Asia 2018), officially known as the 18th Asian Games and also known as Jakarta-Palembang 2018, is a pan-Asian multisport event which were held from 18 August to 2 September 2018 in the Indonesian cities of Jakarta and Palembang. For the first time, the Asian Games were co-hosted in two cities; the Indonesian capital of Jakarta (which hosted the Games for the first time since 1962), and Palembang, the capital of the South Sumatra province. Events were held in and around the two cities including Venues in Bandung and province of West Java and Banten. The opening and closing ceremonies of the Games were held at Gelora Bung Karno Main stadium in Jakarta. For the first time also, eSports and canoe polo were contested as demonstration sports. eSports is expected to be a medal event at the 2022 Asian Games. Around 11,300 athletes competed for 465 events in 40 sports. And at last, China led the medal table with 289 medals (G: 132, S: 92, B: 65) followed by Japan and South Korea. The next Asian Games will be held at Hangzhou in China in 2022. Japanese swimmer Rikako Ikee became the first female athlete to be named the Most Valuable Player (MVP) at this Games after the teenager scooped an unprecedented six gold medals in the Jakarta pool. **INDIA IN ASIAN GAMES 2018: •** *Bajrang Punia,* opened India's gold medal account in men's freestyle wrestling (65 kg). **•** *Vinesh Phogat* created history by becoming the first Indian woman wrestler to win a gold medal at the Asian Games. She won it in women's freestyle 50 kg wrestling event. **•** *Neeraj Chopra,* the flag bearer of this Games, won the gold in javelin event. **•** *Jinson Johnson* claimed a gold medal in the men's 1500 m event. **•** *Rahi Jeevan Sarnobat* became the first Indian woman shooter to win a individual Asian Games gold medal. She won it in women's 25 m pistol category. **•** *India's Tirth Mehta* won a bronze in eSports, which was a demonstration event.

□□□

1908

General Knowledge

www.ingramcontent.com/pod-product-compliance
Lightning Source LLC
Chambersburg PA
CBHW072034150726
47999CB00002B/912